YOU CONVERTED ME

D1056093

YOU CONVERTED ME
The Confessions of St. Augustine

A Modernized Christian Classic

by Augustine of Hippo

Library
Benedictine University Mesa

Modernized translation by Robert J. Edmonson, CJ
Introduction and notes by Rev. Tony Jones

PARACLETE PRESS
BREWSTER, MASSACHUSETTS

2006   First Printing

Copyright © 2006 by Anthony H. Jones for the Introduction and the Notes
Copyright © 2006 by Paraclete Press for the New Translation

ISBN 1-55725-463-X

Unless otherwise indicated, Scripture references are taken from the *Holy Bible, Today's New International Version*™ TNIV ® Copyright © 2001, 2005 by International Bible Society®. All rights reserved worldwide.

Scriptures marked (D-R) are from the Douay-Rheims translation.

Scriptures marked RSV are taken from the *Revised Standard Version* Bible, copyright 1952 [2nd edition, 1971] by the Division of Christian Education of the National Council of the Churches of Christ in the United States of America. Used by permission. All rights reserved.

Library of Congress Cataloging-in-Publication Data
Augustine, Saint, Bishop of Hippo.
   [Confessions. English]
   You converted me : the Confessions of St. Augustine / by
Augustine of Hippo ; modernized translation by Robert J. Edmonson ;
introduction and notes by Tony Jones.
      p. cm.
   ISBN 1-55725-463-X
   1. Augustine, Saint, Bishop of Hippo. 2. Christian
saints—Algeria—Hippo (Extinct city)—Biography. I. Edmonson,
Robert J. II. Title.
   BR65.A6E5 2006b
   270.2092—dc22
                                          2005033052
10 9 8 7 6 5 4 3 2 1

All rights reserved. No portion of this book may be reproduced, stored in an electronic retrieval system, or transmitted in any form or by any means—electronic, mechanical, photocopy, recording, or any other—except for brief quotations in printed reviews, without the prior permission of the publisher.

Published by Paraclete Press
Brewster, Massachusetts
www.paracletepress.com
Printed in the United States of America.

Table of Contents

Introduction

I think it has the makings of a great movie, a classic coming-of-age story. . . .

A boy grows into a man, getting into the kind of mischief that a lot of boys do (messing around with girls, stealing, getting in trouble at school). Meanwhile, his overprotective Christian mother prays fervently for the salvation of his soul, and his unspiritual father pays him little interest. The young man joins a weird, vegetarian cult, and he has a son with his girlfriend.

The young man then flees his mother to study in the big city where he's at once enthralled and disgusted by the parties and carousing around him. All the while, he's tortured internally by his conscience as he searches for "The Truth," worrying that he's going to die before he finds it and as a result be banished to hell. He moves to another city where he falls under the sway of two great Christian men who show him great love and patience, even as he dabbles in another religion.

Finally, accompanied by his best friend, he's driven by his own tormented soul into a garden, where he frantically paces the paths, attacked from all sides by anxiety. He hears the mysterious voice of a child beckoning him, "Take up and read, take up and read," so he returns to the bench where his friend is sitting and opens the biblical book of Romans. He reads one verse, the one that he happens to glance at first, and immediately, calm overcomes his troubled heart, and twenty years worth of doubts suddenly vanish. The young man and his friend run back to his mother. He tells her of his conversion to Christ, and they embrace in joy and weeping.

The Life of Augustine

Quite a story, isn't it? And it's made all the more powerful by the fact that it was written over 1,600 years ago by Aurelius Augustinus, better known as St. Augustine of Hippo, probably the most important theologian in the history of Western Christianity. Augustine was born in the year 354 in the North African town of Tagaste. He was raised by his devoutly Christian (and somewhat overbearing!) mother, Monica, and his pagan father, Patricius, in the city of Carthage. That's where he received his education in rhetoric, which is the study of speech and persuasion.

At age seventeen, in Carthage, Augustine was studying and also partying. He called that city a "cauldron of illicit loves," and he referred to his friends, with whom he often visited the theater, as "the wreckers." During that year, he fell in love with a woman whom he never married, and whose name we don't know. It's sad not to know much about her, because clearly Augustine grew to love her more and more over the years. While they never officially married, they had what today we would call a "common-law marriage."

The next year, when Augustine was eighteen, the young couple had a son, whom they named Adeodatus, which means "God-given." Also that year, Augustine's father died—he was baptized on his deathbed, something many in that time believed would gain him admittance into heaven.

That year, 372, was also a big year for Augustine because he joined the religion of Manicheism. Manicheus, the founder of the religion, lived in Persia (present day Iraq and Iran) from about 210 to about 277. The two other religions in that area of the world that were growing at the time were Christianity and Zoroastrianism, and Manicheus took elements from both into his religious system. He claimed to be the Holy Spirit promised by Jesus in the New Testament, and he founded a religion most notable for its *dualism*. That is, Manicheans (and you might pick this up in Augustine's writings) believed that everything in the world was divided up between good and bad, light and dark. For instance, they believed that vegetables (and all green things) were good, but meat (and red things) were bad; so, obviously, they were vegetarians.

But over his eight or nine years as a Manichean, Augustine became more and more troubled by the teaching of this religion. You'll see in the pages that follow that Augustine was truly a tortured soul until he converted to Christianity. At first, Manicheism helped him to understand all of his sinful desires, because he could blame them on his body, which Manicheans taught was ultimately an evil, material creation. But as time passed, he became less content with these answers, and he started to search for truth elsewhere.

At age twenty, Augustine, his common-law wife, and Adeodatus returned first to Tagaste (where his mother would not let him in the house because he was a Manichean) and then to Carthage, where he opened his own school of rhetoric and continued his study of the Manichean religion. He stayed there for nine years, but several friends wrote him letters, urging him to return to Rome, the capital of the empire—that's where the action was. The little family of three did move, but they snuck away, not telling Monica that they were going!

Just a year after arriving in Rome, Augustine was appointed to a prime teaching post in Milan, a city in northern Italy. By that point, he was truly disillusioned with the religion of Manicheus, and he left it. Instead, he began to study Neoplatonism. This philosophical-religious system taught that there was no such thing as evil in the world, only beings that had attained different levels of perfection. The more that a person could rid himself of bodily appetites (like sex, food, and drink), the more perfection he could attain, and the more perfection he could attain, the more divine he could become. This was an optimistic outlook, and it greatly appealed to Augustine after all of the negativity of Manicheism.

But Augustine came under another influence in Milan, and that was Ambrose, the Christian bishop of that city. Although Augustine writes that the great Ambrose really didn't have time to meet with him for a chat, the still-young Augustine attended church almost every Sunday to hear the bishop speak. At first, Augustine was impressed with Ambrose's rhetorical talent, then with the fact that such a wise man could be a Christian. Finally, Augustine was persuaded by the brilliance of the bishop's sermons that Christianity, in fact, was logical and understandable.

As you will see in the pages that follow, everything came to a head for Augustine in Milan. He realized that his previous religious commitments were false-hood. His mother had pressured him to leave his common-law wife and son to marry a good, Christian girl (but, instead, he started sleeping with another woman!), and he had become convinced that even his career as a public speaker was a farce. In the end, he converted to Christianity, or, as he says it in a prayer to Christ, "You converted me." I don't particularly want to summarize that moment—it's so beautiful that I want you to read it for yourself. And, trust me, it's worth the wait. . . .

Augustine went on to live a long and productive life, even after the tragic deaths of his mother, son, and close friends. He never married or had any more children, but moved back to Hippo, a town in northern Africa, and established a monastery there. He spent the rest of his life writing some of the most powerful and compelling Christian theology and philosophy that's ever been written. When he died in 430 at the age of seventy-six, he had preached over 500 sermons, written 240 letters, and authored over 100 books.

The Confessions

What you're about to read was unprecedented at the time—in fact, this book is the first known autobiography ever written in the Western world. It's not really a diary or a journal, but more of a memoir. It traces Augustine's life from his birth through the age of thirty-three. (While it may sound strange that it covers Augustine's birth because, of course, he couldn't remember it, he does write about it, for it greatly interests him. You see, there were many skeptical philosophers in his day, just like today, who said that we, as human beings, can't know anything with certainty. Augustine argued that although he couldn't remember his birth, he could say with certainty that his parents were his parents. You'll see that he also writes a lot about the fact that his mother cared for him before he could give her any affection back, and he compares this to how God cared for him before he converted to Christianity.)

But, as I was saying, it's an autobiography, and it's written in thirteen "books." The first eight are in this volume, and they take us through his conversion at age thirty-one. Augustine actually didn't start writing the *Confessions* until he was forty-six, and it took him a couple of years to complete the work. When you read his detailed accounts of things that happened to him and how he felt when he was a teenager, you'll discover one of the most amazing aspects of this book and of Augustine's mind: He had an incredible memory. As scholars have studied this book over the centuries, they've been dazzled by Augustine's recall of events.

But why is it called the *Confessions*? Well, first off, because Augustine spends a lot of time confessing his sins in this book, most especially the sins he committed before he became a Christian. You'll see, for instance, a famous section in which he goes on at some length wondering what led him to steal pears from an orchard when he was a boy.

But the reason that he confesses his sins in these pages isn't to cleanse his soul, for he knows that his soul has already been cleansed by his confessing his sins to God and by the love of Christ. No, he confesses his sins in print so that he can make the same point over and over: In spite of Augustine's sinful ways, God had his hand on young Augustine all along. That's why, at many points, Augustine quits telling his story and virtually breaks out in song to God. A related point is that Augustine is sure that God heard the prayers of his faithful mother, Monica, all those years of his wayward youth.

Not only is Augustine confessing his sins, but also he's confessing to the world his faith in Christ. And, most important, he's confessing his love for God. The *Confessions*, in fact, are written to God, as is seen in a famous line from the second paragraph: ". . . our hearts are restless until they rest in you."

Reading Tips

What may be most striking to you as you read this book is how you've experienced many of the same things that Augustine recounts about his years as a child, a teenager, and a young adult. He does naughty things, hangs out with the wrong group of friends, fools around sexually, steals stuff, and causes his mother lots of grief. But more important than *what he does* is *how he feels*. In fact, you may want to pay special attention to what he writes about how he feels, for you may know exactly what he's talking about.

But for all the similarities, it's also important to remember that this book is from another time. An "anachronism" is an artifact, person, or word that seems to belong to another time, and there are indeed some of those in this book. You'll notice, for instance, that Augustine believes that women are physically and psychologically weaker than men, the "frail sex." While we call this sexism today, in Augustine's time, it was commonly thought to be true. When it comes to items like this, I've often written a little note meant to help you get over the hurdle of a strange phrase or obscure reference.

I've also placed notes around some concepts that may be hard to follow, and I try to tip you off a few times when Augustine makes a sharp turn in his writing without using his blinker. Other things that you may be unsure of will come up in the text—if it's a word you've never seen, I strongly encourage you to look it up (you may see it on the SAT!), and if it's a strange name or an obscure reference, write a note in the back of the book and Google it later.

Finally, if you're anything like me, it takes you a while to get into the language when you start read-ing a Shakespearean play. Well, the same goes here: Just power through the first three or four pages, and you'll start to get the hang of it. You can always go back and read them again later. Remember that

Augustine is writing with God as the intended audience, and that he will occasionally break into explicit (and beautiful) prayers. And feel free to read this book with a pen or a highlighter in your hand to underline some of the beautiful, poignant, and powerful things that Augustine wrote more than sixteen centuries ago.

Tony Jones
Edina, Minnesota

Chapter One

Infancy to Age Fifteen

"Lord, you are great, and most worthy of praise" (Psalm 48:1). "Your power is mighty, and your understanding has no limit" (Psalm 147:5). We want to praise you; we—who are only small particles of your creation—yes, we, though with us we carry our mortality, the evidence of our sin, the evidence that you resist the proud. We are only particles of your creation, but in spite of that we praise you.

You awake us to delight in your praise; for you made us for yourself, and our hearts are restless until they rest in you.

Allow me, Lord, to know and understand which of these is most important: to call on you or to praise you. And again: to know you or to call on you. For who can call on you without knowing you? One who doesn't know you might call on you as if you were other than you are. Or do we perhaps call on you so that we may know you? "How, then, can they call on the one they have not believed in? . . . And how can they hear without someone preaching to them?" (Romans 10:14).

 When you see quotation marks, most often they show a quote from the Bible. They may also indicate a quote from a poet.

And "Let the hearts of those who seek the Lord rejoice" (Psalm 105:3). Because those who seek will find him, and those who find will praise him. Let me seek you, Lord, by calling on you, and call on you believing in you, because someone has preached you to us. My faith calls on you, Lord: the faith you've given me, the faith you've breathed into me through your Son's being born in the flesh, through the ministry of the preacher.

But how will I call on my God, my God and Lord? Because when I call on him, I ask him to come to me. And what room is there in me, where my God can come—God who made heaven and earth? Is there anything in me, Lord, my God, that can contain you? Do heaven and earth—which you've made, and in which you made me—contain you? Or, since nothing could exist without you, does everything that exists contain you? Why, then, do I ask that you come into me, since I, too, exist—I who couldn't exist if you weren't in me? Why do I say this? Because even if I were in hell, you would be there as well. For "if I make my bed in the depths, you are there" (Psalm 139:8). I couldn't exist then, my God, couldn't exist at all, unless you were in me. Or should I say, I couldn't exist unless I were in you, "from whom and through whom and to whom are all things" (Romans 11:36).

Even so, Lord, even so. Where do I call you to come, since I'm in you? Or from where can you enter into me? Where, beyond heaven and earth, could I go that my God, who has said, "I fill heaven and earth" (Jeremiah 23:24), might come into me?

 Remember in the introduction when I said that you might have to power through the first few pages? Well, I'm back to give you a pep talk. This opening section is a long string of rhetorical questions; that is, questions that don't really have answers. Rather than getting bogged down in them, just keep reading and try to get a feel for what Augustine is doing.

Do heaven and earth then contain you, since you fill them? Or, do you fill them and yet overflow, since they can't contain you? And where, when heaven and earth are filled, do you pour out what remains of yourself? Or, is there no need for you who contain all things to be contained by anything, since those things you fill, you fill by containing them?

The vessels that you fill don't sustain you, since even if they were broken, you wouldn't be poured out. And when you're poured out on us, you're not cast down, but we're lifted up. You're not dispersed, but we're drawn together. But as you fill all things, do you also fill them with your whole self? Or, since all things can't contain you completely, do they contain part of you? Do they all contain the same part at once, or does each have its own proper part—with greater things having more, and smaller things having less? If this is so, then is one part of you greater, and another part of you less? Or are you completely everywhere, while nothing may completely contain you?

What are you then, my God—what, but the Lord God? "For who is God besides the LORD? And who is the Rock except our God?" (Psalm 18:31). Most high, most excellent, most powerful, most mighty, most merciful, and most just; most hidden, but most present; most beautiful, and most strong; stable, but mysterious; unchangeable, but changing all things; never new, never old; making all things new and bringing age upon the proud, though they don't know it; ever working, but ever at rest; still gathering, but lacking nothing; sustaining, filling, and protecting; creating, nourishing, and maturing; seeking, but possessing all things.

You love without passion; you're jealous without anxiety; you repent, but have no sorrow; you're angry, but serene; you change your ways, but your plans are unchanged; you recover what you find, having never lost it; you're never in need, but you rejoice in gain; you're never covetous, but you require interest. You receive over and above, so that you may owe—yet who has anything that isn't yours? You pay debts, but you owe nothing; you remit debts, but you lose nothing. And what have I now said, my God, my life, my holy One—what is this I have said? Or what does anyone say when they speak of you? Nevertheless, those who keep silent should be on their guard, since those who say the most are like those who can't speak.

Oh, how will I find rest in you? Who will send you into my heart to flood it, so that I may forget my troubles and embrace you, my only good? What are you to me? In your pity, teach me to speak. What am I to you that you demand my love, and if I don't give it, you are angry with me and threaten me with great sorrows? Is it then, a slight sorrow not to love you? Oh, no! For your mercies' sake, Lord my God, tell me what you are to me. "Say to me, 'I am your salvation'" (Psalm 35:3). When I hear this word, let me run and lay hold of you. Don't hide your face from me. Let me see it, even if I die, for I surely will die if I don't see it.

The house of my soul is narrow. Enlarge it, so that you may enter it. It's in ruins! Repair it! It has things in it that would offend your eyes. I confess and know it. But who will cleanse it, or to whom will I cry, but to you? Lord, forgive my willful sins (Psalm 19:13) and spare your servant from the hands of the enemy (Psalm 31:8). "I trusted in the LORD when I [spoke]" Psalm 116:10. Lord, you know. Haven't I confessed my transgressions to you, and you, my God, have forgiven the guilt of my sin? (Psalm 31:5). I don't want to dispute with you, who are the Truth (Job 9:3, John 14:6). I'm afraid to deceive myself, because my gross immorality might lie against itself. So I don't want to dispute with you, because "If you, LORD, kept a record of sins, Lord, who could stand?" (Psalm 130:3).

OK, you made it. Now stop, take a breath, and think back—what do you think that Augustine was up to with all of those questions?

But allow me to speak before your mercy, me— "dust and ashes" (Genesis 18:27). Allow me to speak, for I speak to your mercy and not to the contempt of others. Perhaps you too despise me, but when you turn to me, you'll have compassion on me. For what would I say, Lord my God, but that I don't know where I came from into this—should I call it *dying life*, or *living death?* But, as I was told by my earthly parents, out of whose substance you fashioned me (I don't remember it), the comforts of your compassion sustained me. Then I received the comfort of human milk; my mother and my nurses didn't fill their own breasts, but you gave the nourishment of my infancy through them, according to your rules and that liberal generosity of yours that lies beneath all things.

You also caused me to want no more than you provided. And those who nourished me gave me willingly what you gave them, for they, with a heaven-taught affection, willingly gave me what you had abundantly supplied. It was good for them that my good should come from them, though in truth it wasn't really *from* them but *by* them, for all good things are from you, God, and all my health comes from you. This is what I've learned since you declared yourself to me through your blessings, both those that are within me and those that are outside of me, which you've given to me. At one time I only knew how to suck, to be satisfied when comfortable, and to cry when in pain—nothing more.

 Augustine is writing about his own infancy, not because he can remember it, but because he has seen many infants and can assume that he was similar to them.

Afterward I began to smile, first when I was sleeping, then when I was awake. I was told this about myself, and I believe it, for we see the same thing in other infants. So, little by little, I realized where I was and wanted to express my desires to those who could satisfy them, since I couldn't! And that's because my wants were inside me and they were outside me, and couldn't by any faculty of their own enter my soul. So I randomly flung around my arms and legs and my voice, making the few signs that I could, suggesting (though very inadequately) by signs or sounds what it was I wanted. And when I wasn't feeling satisfied— because what I wanted either wasn't understood or wasn't good for me—I got annoyed at my elders and angry with those who didn't owe me anything, because they weren't serving me, and I took revenge on them by crying. That's how I've learned infants to be by watching them, and I've found out that I was the same way myself.

But I was an infant a long time ago, and yet I live on. But you, Lord, live forever and in you nothing dies, since before the foundation of the world and before all that can be called "before," you are, and you are God and Lord of all that you've created. With you, who are unchanging forever, live the first causes of all things that pass away, the unchanging sources of all things that change, the eternal reasons of all things that lack reason and are limited by time.

Tell me, Lord, I who humbly and earnestly ask you. You who are all-merciful, tell your miserable one—tell me: Did my infancy follow another age of mine that died before it? Was it in another age that I spent within my mother's womb? I've heard something about that and I've seen pregnant women for myself. And then what about before that life, God, my joy? Was I anywhere or anybody? No one can tell me this—not my father or mother, not experience, not other people, not my own memory. Perhaps you laugh at me for asking such things, and you invite me to praise you and acknowledge you for what I do know.

Do we exist before we are conceived in our mother's body? Augustine asks this question here, but he admits that we can never know the answer.

I give you thanks, Lord of heaven and earth, and praise you for my first being and my infancy, about which I remember nothing. You've appointed that humankind should learn much about themselves from others and believe many things on the authority of frail women.

Like me, you may cringe when you see Augustine refer to women as "frail." He's not being sexist, exactly, because in his day it was commonly believed that women were more emotional and therefore psychologically and physically weaker than men. Thankfully, we know better than that today, but Augustine was a product of his times, so I suggest we give him the benefit of the doubt here.

Even then I had life and being, and at the close of my infancy I was already looking for ways to make my feelings known to others. Where could such a creature come from, Lord, but from you, or will any of us be skillful enough to create ourselves? Or can any stream be found anywhere else that brings being and life into us, except this, that you, Lord, have made us, with whom being and life are one, because you're supremely being and life? For you are most high and you don't change.

And today doesn't come to a close in you, and yet it does come to a close in you, because all such things are also in you. For they would have no way even to pass away unless you sustained them. And since "the heavens . . . will perish, but you remain" (Psalm 101:25-26), your years are like an ever-present today. How many of our years and our fathers' years have flowed away through your today, and received from it their measure and shape of being? And still others to come will receive the shape of their degree of being and will pass away. But you're still the same, and all tomorrows and what is beyond them, and all yesterdays and what is behind them, you make to be in your today. What does it matter to me, even if none of us can understand this? Let's still be glad and say, "What is this?" (Exodus 16:15). Let's be content by not understanding to find you, rather than by understanding not to find you.

Hear me, God! It's only because of the sin of humankind that we speak this way, and you have compassion on us, for you made us, but you didn't make sin in us. Who reminds me of the sins of my infancy? For in your sight, no one is free from sin, not even the infant who has lived for only one day upon the earth (see Job 14:1–4).

Who reminds me? Doesn't each little infant in whom I see what I don't remember about myself? What was my sin then? Is it that I cried for the breast? For if I were to cry that way now for food suitable to my present age, I would be laughed at and scolded. What I did then deserved scolding, but since I couldn't understand scolding, custom and reason prevented people from scolding me. For as we grow, we root out and cast away such habits.

Now, even if a person prunes trees or bushes, no one knowingly throws away what is good. Or was it good then, even for a time, to cry for what, if it were given to me, would be hurtful—to bitterly resent that those free persons, elders—even my own parents who gave me birth—didn't serve me? That many others besides, wiser than I, didn't obey the beckoning of my good pleasure? That I did my best to strike and hurt because my commands weren't obeyed, commands that would have been only harmful to me if they'd been carried out? Then in the weakness of an infant's body, not its will, lies its innocence.

I've seen and known an infant to be jealous, even though it couldn't speak. It turned pale and looked bitterly at its foster-brother. Who doesn't know this to be true? Mothers and nurses tell you that they appease these things by all kinds of remedies. Is it innocence when the fountain of milk is flowing in rich abundance, not to allow another to share it, though the other one needs the nourishment to sustain its life? We look leniently on all this, not because we fail to recognize the presence and degree of the evils, but because they will disappear as age increases. For although they are allowed in infancy, the very same tempers are utterly intolerable when they appear in an older person.

Lord my God, who gave life to my infancy by furnishing the body you gave me with senses, knitting its limbs together, shaping its proportions and implanting in me all the impulses necessary for maintaining the integrity and safety of a living being—you command me to praise you in these things, "to praise the LORD and make music to your name, O Most High" (Psalm 92:1). For you are God, almighty and good, even if you had done nothing but these things that no one but you could do. You alone made all things, most Fair One, and you make all things fair; and by your law you order all things.

This period of my life, then, Lord, of which I have no memory, which I take on others' word and which I guess from observing other infants—true though the guess may be—I don't care to reckon as a part of my life that I live in this world. For it's hidden from me in the shadows of forgetfulness no less than the time I spent in my mother's womb. But if "I was sinful at birth, sinful from the time my mother conceived me" (Psalm 51:5), where, I pray, my God, where, Lord, or when, was I, your servant, innocent? But I pass that period by. What do I now have to do with that period of which I have no memories?

 One of Augustine's major contributions to Christian theology was the doctrine of Original Sin, and you see it in this paragraph. This is the (somewhat controversial) belief that, because of the sin of Adam and Eve, all human beings are born sinful and in need of salvation before they even commit a sin of their own.

Passing on from infancy, I came to boyhood, or rather it came to me. My infancy didn't depart (where did it go?) and yet it was no more. For I was no longer a speechless infant, but a chattering boy. This I do remember, and I've since observed how I learned to speak.

My elders didn't teach me words by any particular method (as a little later they taught me other things). But when I was unable to say all I wanted and to whomever I wanted by whimpering and broken sounds and various gestures that I used to enforce my wishes, I myself began to repeat the sounds in my memory according to the understanding that you, my God, gave me. When they called anything by name and turned toward it as they spoke, I saw and gathered that the object they were pointing out was called by that name. And I understood by their gestures that they meant this thing and nothing else, movements that are the natural language, so to speak, of all peoples, expressed by facial expressions, glances of the eyes, movements of the arms and legs, and tones of the voice, indicating the feelings of the mind as it searches for, gets, rejects or avoids certain things.

And so by frequently hearing words as they occurred in various sentences, I gradually gathered what they meant. Having formed my mouth to make these sounds, I could then give voice to my will. Therefore I exchanged with those about me these current expressions of our wants, and so advanced deeper into the stormy fellowship of human life, still subject to parental authority and the bidding of my elders.

God, my God! What miseries and mockeries I now experienced, when obedience to my teachers was set before me as proper to my boyhood so that I might prosper in this world and excel in the knowledge of speech that would gain the praise of other people and deceitful riches. After that, I was put in school to get learning, the usefulness of which I couldn't imagine (useless as I was), and yet if I was idle in my studies, I was flogged! For our ancestors considered this to be the right way, and many, passing the same way before us, had laid out the weary paths through which we were obliged to pass, multiplying labor and grief on the children of Adam.

But, Lord, we found that people prayed to you, and we learned from them to think of you according to our abilities, to be some Great One who, though hidden from our senses, could hear and help us. So I began, even as a boy, to pray to you, my help and refuge. And I let my tongue freely call on you, praying to you, even though I was small, with no small earnestness, that I might not be flogged at school. And when you didn't hear me, my elders, yes, my own parents who certainly wished me no harm, laughed at my small wounds, which at that point were a source of great and grievous distress to me.

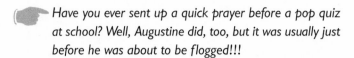

Have you ever sent up a quick prayer before a pop quiz at school? Well, Augustine did, too, but it was usually just before he was about to be flogged!!!

Is there anyone, Lord, who is bound to you with such greatness of soul and with so strong an affection (there is a sort of stupidity that may do that much)— is there anyone who is endowed with so great a courage from clinging devoutly to you, that they can think lightly of racks and hooks and other tortures? For throughout the whole world people pray fervently to be saved from such tortures. Can they ridicule people who are afraid of them as bitterly as our parents ridiculed the torments that we suffered from our teachers in boyhood? For we didn't fear our torments any less, nor did we pray less to you to escape them. And yet we sinned in writing, reading, or studying less than was required of us. For we weren't short on memory or ability, Lord, of which, by your will, we possessed enough for our age. But the only thing we took great pleasure in was playing, and for this we were punished by those who were doing the same things themselves.

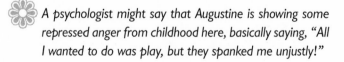

A psychologist might say that Augustine is showing some repressed anger from childhood here, basically saying, "All I wanted to do was play, but they spanked me unjustly!"

But older people's idleness is called business, while boys who do the same are punished by those same elders; and yet no one expresses pity, either boys or adults. For will any one of good sense approve of my being whipped because as a boy I played ball, and so I made less progress in studies that I was to learn only so that, as a man, I might play more shameful games? And what else was my tutor doing who beat me, who, if he was defeated in some trifling controversy with his fellow tutor, was more bitter and angry than I was when I was beaten in a game of ball by a playmate?

And yet I sinned in this, Lord God, Creator and Disposer of all things in nature (but of sin only the Disposer). Lord my God, I sinned acting against the commands of my parents and of my teachers. For what they, with whatever motive, wanted me to learn, I might have put to good use later on. But I disobeyed, not because I had chosen a better way, but from love of playing. I loved having the honor of victory in my contests, and of having my ears tickled with fables so that they might itch for more.

The same curiosity burned in my eyes more and more for the shows and sports of adults. Those who gave these shows were held in such esteem that almost everyone wished the same for their children, and they were very willing for the children to be flogged if these very games kept them from their studies by which they wanted them to reach the point of being teachers to others.

Look down with compassion on these things, Lord, and deliver us who call upon you now. Deliver those, too, who don't call on you, so that they may call on you and so that you may deliver them.

Library
Benedictine University Mesa

As a boy, then, I had heard of eternal life promised us through the humility of the Lord our God stooping to our pride. Even from the womb of my mother, who greatly hoped in you, I was signed with the mark of his cross and seasoned with his salt.

Here Augustine recounts the first of two fevers that almost killed him. His mother, Monica, fervently prayed for him, and she almost had him baptized on his deathbed, a common practice at the time.

You saw, Lord, how at one time when yet a boy I was suddenly seized with pains in the stomach and was near death. You saw, my God, for you were my Keeper, with what eagerness of mind and with what faith I asked for the baptism of Christ, your Anointed One, my God and Lord, due to the devoutness of my own mother and of your Church, the mother of us all. At that time, my mother was very anxious, since she worked more lovingly in labor for my salvation than during my natural birth. She would have provided for my cleansing initiation by your health-giving sacraments, confessing you, Lord Jesus, for the remission of sins, if I hadn't suddenly recovered. And so, because I would be further polluted if I were to live, my cleansing through baptism was deferred, because the defilements of sin would bring greater and more perilous guilt after that washing.

I already believed at that time, with my mother and the whole household except my father. Yet he didn't overcome the power of my mother's devoutness in me so as to prevent me from believing in Christ. The fact that he didn't yet believe didn't make me think that I shouldn't. For it was her earnest concern that you, my God, should be my Father rather than he. In this you enabled her to overcome her husband: Though the better of the two, she deferred to him in obedience because in this she obeyed your commandment as well.

I earnestly ask you, my God, for I would like to know, if it's your will, for what purpose was my baptism then deferred? Was it for my good that the reins were loosened on me, so to speak, for me to sin? Or is it actually that they weren't slackened at all? If not, why does it still echo in my ears to hear it said from all sides, "Leave him alone, let him do what he wants, for he hasn't been baptized yet"? But when it comes to bodily health, no one says, "Let him be wounded even more seriously, for he isn't healed yet." How much better, then, would it have been for me to have been healed spiritually at once. And then, by my friends' diligence and my own, my soul's recovered health would have been kept safe in your keeping who gave it! My mother foresaw these things and preferred to expose the unformed, unregenerate clay to them rather than the very image itself after it was made.

In my childhood, which was less dangerous for me than my adolescence, I had no love of learning and hated to be forced to learn. Yet I was forced to do it, and this was good for me, though I didn't do well. For I wouldn't have learned unless I was compelled. But no one does well against his will, even though what he does may be good. Yet those who forced me didn't do well either; no, the good that came to me was from you, my God. For they were totally uncaring of how I should use what they forced me to learn, except to satisfy the inordinate desire for shameful glory.

But you, by whom "the very hairs of our head are all numbered" (Matthew 10:30), used for my good the error of all those who urged me to learn. And my own error in my unwillingness to learn, you used for my punishment—a fitting penalty for so small a boy and so great a sinner. So by the instruments of those who didn't do well, you did well for me; and by my own sin you justly punished me. For you have appointed, and it is so, that every inordinate affection should be its own punishment.

 Here he's making the point that sin contains its own punishment, and rarely does a punishment need to be added.

But why did I so hate the Greek language, which I studied as a boy? I don't yet fully know the answer. For I loved Latin—not what my first teachers taught me, but what the so-called grammarians teach. For those first lessons—reading, writing, and arithmetic—I thought were as great a burden and punishment as any Greek studies.

And yet where did all this come from, too, but from the sin and vanity of this life? Because I was "but flesh, a passing breeze that does not return" (Psalm 78:39). For those primary lessons were better, certainly, because they were more certain. By them I achieved and still retain the ability to read written material, and the ability to write what I want.

The Aeneid *is a great, epic poem written by Virgil in the first century* BC. *It tells the legendary story of Aeneas, a warrior and sailor from Troy who sails with his army to the Italian peninsula and, with the help of the gods, defeats the people who live there and founds Rome. Before he gets there, however, his ships dock at Carthage in Northern Africa, where Dido is the queen. She throws a great banquet for Aeneas and his men, and in the course of the evening, she falls madly in love with him. Although it's tempting to stay with Dido, Aeneas knows that his destiny lies ahead, and he leaves in the morning. Deep in grief, Dido curses Aeneas and commits suicide by throwing herself on a burning funeral pyre, the smoke from which Aeneas sees as he sails away.*

On the other hand, I was forced to learn about the wanderings of Aeneas, forgetting my own wanderings, and to weep for Dido, who was dead because she killed herself for love. While at the same time, with dry eyes I tolerated my wretched self dying among these things, far from you, God of my life.

What is more pitiful than a miserable person who doesn't pity himself, weeping over the death of Dido for her love of Aeneas, but shedding no tears over his own death and not loving you, God, Light of my heart, Bread of my inmost soul, Power that weds my mind with my inmost thought?

 While "fornication" officially refers to two unmarried persons having sex, Augustine uses the word more symbolically here. He means that he was overly consumed with the world and forsaking the one who loves him most, namely, Christ.

I didn't love you, and I committed fornication against you, and all those around me, who were doing the same, echoed, "Well done! Well done!" For the friendship of this world is fornication against you, and "Well done! Well done!" echoes on till one is ashamed not to be such a person.

And for all this I didn't weep, although I wept for Dido, killed as she attempted to find death at the point of a sword. But I myself was searching for the extremest and lowest level of your creatures, having forgotten you, dirt sinking to dirt. And if I were told not to read all this, I was distressed that I wasn't allowed to read what distressed me. Madness like this is considered more honorable and more fruitful learning than the instruction by which I learned to read and write.

But now, my God, shout aloud in my soul and let your truth tell me, "It isn't so! That first study was far better!" For I would rather forget the wanderings of Aeneas and all such things than how to read and write.

Over the entrance of the Grammar School a veil is hung, it's true, but this isn't so much a sign of honor of the mysteries taught in them as a covering for error. Don't let those whom I no longer fear shout out against me while I confess whatever my soul desires to you, my God. Let them agree in condemning my evil ways, so that I may love your good ways.

Let neither buyers nor sellers of grammar education shout out against me. For if I question them as to whether Aeneas came once to Carthage, as the poet tells, the less educated will reply that they don't know; the more educated, that he never did. But if I ask with what letters the name "Aeneas" is written, everyone who has learned this will answer me rightly, in accordance with the conventional understanding people have settled on as to these signs. If, again, I ask which might be forgotten with the least detriment to the concerns of life—reading and writing, or these poetic fictions, who can't see what all must answer who haven't wholly forgotten themselves? I got it wrong then, when as a boy I preferred those vain and useless studies to the more profitable ones, or rather loved the one and hated the other. "One and one are two; two and two are four." This to me was a hateful sing-song; but such vanities as the wooden horse full of armed men and the burning of Troy and the "ghostly image" of Creusa [Aeneas's wife] were a most pleasant but useless spectacle.

Here's some more ancient literary imagery that you don't have to get too hung up on, but you may be familiar with the famous story of the Trojan horse: In a trick, the Greek army left a giant wooden horse outside the walls of Troy. Thinking it was a peace offering, the Trojans brought it inside the city walls, but after nightfall, hundreds of Greek warriors climbed out of it and ransacked the city.

Why then did I hate the Greek classics, which have the same kind of tales? For Homer also skillfully wove the same fictions, and is more sweetly useless, yet he was disagreeable to my boyish taste. And so I suppose Virgil would be to Greek children, if they were forced to learn him as I was forced to learn Homer. So here's the real difficulty of learning a foreign language, merged, so to speak, with all the sweetness of the Greek fable. For I didn't understand one word of it, and to make me understand I was urged vehemently with cruel threats and punishments.

There was a time, of course, when as an infant I didn't know any Latin. But this language I acquired without fear or torment, by simple observation, accompanied by the caresses of my nurses and the banter of those who smiled at me, and the sportiveness of those who encouraged me. I learned all this without any pressure of punishment, for my own heart urged me to build its own impressions, which I could only do by learning words—not of those who taught me, but of those who talked to me, and into whose ears I also brought whatever thoughts I had.

No doubt then, free curiosity has more influence in our learning these things than enforcement by fear. But this enforcement restrains the overflowing of unrestrained freedom. Your laws, God, your laws—from the teacher's cane to the martyr's trials—are able to turn bitterness into a wholesome thing, and call us back to yourself from the insidious pleasures that lure us from you.

Hear my prayer, Lord; don't let my soul collapse under your discipline. Don't let me grow weary in confessing before you all your mercies by which you've saved me from my most evil ways. I want you to become sweet to me above all the seductions that I once followed. I want to love you entirely and clasp your hand with my whole heart. I want you to still deliver me from every temptation, even to the end. Lord, my King and my God, let whatever useful thing I learned as a child be for your service, and for your service whatever I speak, write, read, or count. For you granted me your discipline while I was learning unproductive things. You've forgotten my sin in taking delight in those worthless pursuits. Indeed, I learned many a useful word in them, but these may be better learned in things that aren't unproductive; and that's the safe path for youths to walk in.

But woe to you, stream of human custom! Who can stay your course? How long will it be before you're dried up? How long will you carry the children of Eve into that huge and hideous ocean that even those who are embarked on the Tree can scarcely pass over?

 When Augustine refers to "the children of Eve" he means all of us; when he says that we are "embarked on the Tree" he is referring to the Cross, which is our new Noah's ark.

Didn't I read in you about Jupiter the thunderer and adulterer? Without a doubt, he couldn't be both of these things, except to have the real adultery supposedly sanctioned and catered to by the pretended thunder. And now, which of our gowned teachers lends a sober ear to one who from their own school cries out, "These were Homer's fictions; he transferred human things to the gods; I wish that he had transferred divine things to us"?

 Here Augustine is re-interpreting the classic tales of Homer, saying that Homer inappropriately attributed divine characteristics to sinful human beings.

Yet it would be more truthful if he said, "Homer did indeed make all this up; but he ascribed divine attributes to wicked people, so that crimes might not be reckoned as crimes, and so that whoever commits them might appear to imitate the heavenly gods, not forsaken humankind!"

And yet, hellish stream of custom, into you are cast the sons and daughters of men and women with rich rewards for learning such things. And much is made of it when this is going on in the Forum in view of laws that grant salaries in addition to the scholars' payments. And you lash upon your rocks and roar, "Here words are learned! Here eloquence is attained, essential to gain your ends or to persuade people to your way of thinking." So in truth we would never have known such words as "golden shower," "bosom," "intrigue," "temples of the heavens," or other words in that passage, if Terence hadn't brought a good-for-nothing youth on the stage to set up Jupiter as his example of lewdness.

> *Viewing a picture, where the tale was drawn,*
> *Of Jove's descending in a golden shower*
> *To Danae's bosom . . . with a woman's intrigue.*

 Over the next few pages, when you see italics in stanzas like this, Augustine is quoting an ancient poem. (Terence lived from 195 to 159 BC.)

And then notice how he excites himself to lust as if by celestial authority, when he says,

> *Great Jove,*
> *Who shakes the heaven's highest temples with his*
> *   thunder,*
> *And I, poor mortal man, do not do the same?*
> *I did it, and with all my heart I did it.*

The words aren't learned one bit more easily as a result of their being depraved; but because of them the depravity is perpetuated with more confidence. Not that I blame the words. They are, so to speak, choice and precious vessels. But intoxicated teachers poured out the wine of error to us in them. And if we, too, didn't drink, we were beaten, and we didn't have a sober judge to whom we could appeal. Yet, my God, in whose presence I now can remember this without being hurt by it, all this, unhappily, I learned willingly with great delight, and for this I was called a promising boy.

Bear with me, my God, while I speak a little about those talents you've bestowed on me, and about what foolishness I wasted them on. For I was given a task, troublesome enough to my soul (in hope of praise or fear of shame or punishment), to speak the words of Juno [queen of the gods and Jupiter's wife], as she raged and mourned that she couldn't

Bar off Italy
From all approaches of the Trojan prince.

I had learned that Juno never uttered these words, but we were forced to wander in the paths of these poetic fictions and say in prose much of what the poet expressed in verse. And the one whose speaking showed most the passions of rage and grief, and best reproduced the dignity of the character, was most applauded. What is it to me, my true Life, my God, that my recitation on this subject was applauded above that of many of my own age and class? Isn't all this smoke and wind?

And was there nothing else on which I could exercise my wit and my tongue? Your praises, Lord, your praises might have supported the tender shoots of my heart by your Scriptures, so that it might not have been dragged away among these empty trifles, a shameful prey for the fowls of the air. For there are more ways than one of sacrificing to the fallen angels.

What wonder is it that I was carried away to vanity and strayed from you, my God, when people were set before me as models, who, if in talking about some action of theirs that wasn't evil in itself, they committed some incorrect use of language or breach of etiquette, and being severely criticized, became embarrassed. But when they made a full and ornate oration in well-ordered words, telling of their own disordered life, and were applauded for it, they boasted. These things you see, Lord, and you hold your peace, since you are "compassionate and gracious, slow to anger, abounding in love" (Psalm 103:8). Will you keep silent forever?

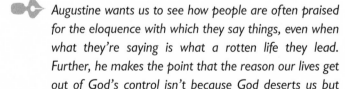 *Augustine wants us to see how people are often praised for the eloquence with which they say things, even when what they're saying is what a rotten life they lead. Further, he makes the point that the reason our lives get out of God's control isn't because God deserts us but because we stray from God.*

And even now you draw out of this vast, immeasurable chasm the soul that searches for you, that thirsts for your pleasures, whose heart says to you, "'Seek his face!' Your face, LORD, I will seek" (Psalm 27:8).

I was far from your face, for darkened affections mean separation from you. For it isn't by our feet or change of place that we either leave you or return to you. That younger [prodigal] son (see Luke 15:11–32) didn't look out for horses or chariots or ships, fly with visible wings, or journey by the motion of his legs, so that he might waste all he was given in riotous living in a far country at his departure. You were a loving Father when you gave, and more loving to him when he returned empty. So then the true distance from your face lies in lustful—that is, in darkened—passions.

Observe, Lord, God; yes, look patiently, as you're known to do, how carefully the children of men and women observe the conventional rules of letters and syllables received from those who spoke prior to them, yet neglect the eternal rules of everlasting salvation received from you. So true is this that a teacher or student of the laws of pronunciation that have been handed down to us will offend others more by saying "'uman being" without the "h" in violation of the laws of grammar, than if they, a human being, hated another human being in violation of your law. As if indeed, any enemy could be more destructive than the hatred with which they are incensed against the other, or could wound more deeply the one they persecute than they wound their own heart by their hostility. In truth, there is no knowledge of letters so inborn as the writing of our conscience, that they are doing to another what they would hate to receive from another.

How mysterious are your ways, God. You alone are great, you who sit silent on high and by an unwearied law dispense punishing blindness to unlawful desires. In trying to gain the reputation of eloquence, a person standing before a human judge, surrounded by a human throng, giving vent to angry disapproval of his enemy with the fiercest hatred, will take the greatest care not to let his tongue slip into grammatical error, for fear of murdering the word "human," but pays no attention to whether, through the fury of his spirit, he murders the real human being.

These were the customs in the midst of which I, an unhappy boy, was cast, and it was on this stage that I was more afraid of committing an incorrect use of language than, having committed one, to envy those who hadn't. These things I declare and confess to you, my God; for these things I was applauded by those whom I then thought it my whole duty to please. For I didn't perceive the deep hole of abomination into which I was cast away from your eyes. In your eyes, who could be more infamous than I already was, displeasing even those who were like me, deceiving with innumerable lies my tutor, my teachers, and my parents from love of play, the desire to see stage shows, and a stage-struck restlessness to copy them?

I also stole from my parents' cellar and table, enslaved by greed, or in order to give something to boys who sold me their playthings, which all the while they liked as little as I did. In these games, too, I often tried to gain dishonest victories, dominated as I was by a conceited desire for first place. And what could I tolerate the least in others or, when I detected it, criticize so fiercely, than the very thing I was doing to others? And if I was detected, and I, too, was reprimanded, I chose to quarrel rather than to yield.

Is this the innocence of childhood? Not so, Lord, not so; I ask your mercy, my God. For these same sins, as we grow older, these very sins are transferred from tutors and teachers, from nuts and balls and sparrows, to magistrates and kings, to gold, and lands, and slaves, in the same way that severe punishments take the place of the cane that teachers use to flog their students. It was then the low status of childhood that you, our King, commended as the badge of humility, when you said, "The kingdom of heaven belongs to such as these" (Matthew 19:14).

Yet Lord, Creator and Ruler of the universe, most excellent and good, thanks would have been due to you even if you had destined me only for childhood. For even then I had being, I lived, and I felt. And even then I was concerned for the care of my own well-being—a trace of the mysterious unity that I was derived from. I guarded by intuition the wholeness of my senses, and in these insignificant pursuits, and also in my thoughts on trivial things, I learned to take pleasure in truth. I hated to be deceived, had a vigorous memory, was gifted with the power of speech, was soothed by friendship, and avoided sorrow, meanness, and ignorance. In so small a being, wasn't this wonderful—even praiseworthy? All are gifts from my God; I didn't give them to myself; and they're good. Taken together, they constitute my "self."

The one who made me, then, is good, and he is my Good. I'll rejoice before him for every good gift I enjoyed as a boy. For this is where my sin lay: that I searched for pleasures, honors, and truths in God's creatures rather than in God—in myself and the rest—and so I fell headlong into sorrows, troubles, and errors. Thanks be to you, my joy, my glory, and my confidence, my God; thanks be to you for all your gifts. But do preserve them for me. For in so doing, you'll preserve me, and those things that you've given me will be developed and perfected, and I'll be with you. For my very being comes from you.

Chapter Two
The Purpose of These Confessions

I'll now call to mind my past foulness and the fleshly corruptions of my soul, not because I love them, but so that I may love you, my God.

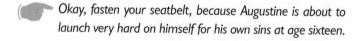 *Okay, fasten your seatbelt, because Augustine is about to launch very hard on himself for his own sins at age sixteen.*

For love of your love I'm doing this, reviewing my most wicked ways in the very bitterness of my memory, so that you may grow sweeter to me. You are sweetness that never fails, delightful and abiding Sweetness, gathering me again from my depravity in which I was torn to shreds while I was alienated from you, the one Good. I wasted myself among a multiplicity of things. For I burned in my youth to take my fill of hell, and ran wild into rank profusion of various and dark loves. My beauty consumed away, and I was rotten in your eyes, pleasing myself and wanting to please others.

And what was it that I delighted in, but to love and be loved? But I didn't keep within the limits of love—of mind to mind, friendship's bright boundary. Out of the muddy strong desire of the flesh and the bubblings of youth, mists fumed up that clouded and overcast my heart, so that I couldn't discern the clear brightness of love from the fog of lustfulness. But confusedly boiling inside, and hurrying my reckless youth over the precipice of unholy desire, I sank in a gulf of shameful and scandalous wickedness.

Your fury hung over me, but I didn't know it. I had grown deaf to the clanking of the chain of my mortality, the punishment of the pride of my soul. I strayed further from you, and you left me alone. I was tossed about, wasted, dissipated, and I boiled over in my sexual liaisons. But you held your peace, you who are only too recently my joy! You held your peace, and I wandered further and further from you into more and more fruitless seed-plots of sorrows, with a proud depression of spirit and a restless weariness.

How I wish that someone had regulated my disorder and turned to some good the passing beauties of these, the least exalted things of your creation! I wish that someone had given boundaries to their delight for me, so that the urges of my youth might have cast themselves on the marriage shore if they couldn't be calmed, and kept them within the confines of a family, as your law prescribes, Lord! For this is the way you form the offspring of this our death, and are able with a gentle hand to blunt the thorns by which we were excluded from your paradise. Your almighty power isn't far from us, even when we're far from you.

But I should have heeded more carefully the voice from the clouds that said, "But those who marry will face many troubles in this life, and I want to spare you this" (1 Corinthians 7:28), and, "It is good for a man not to have sexual relations with a woman" (1 Corinthians 7:1). And further, "An unmarried man is concerned about the Lord's affairs—how he can please the Lord. But a married man is concerned about the affairs of this world—how he can please his wife" (1 Corinthians 7:32-33). I should have listened more attentively to these words and, being separated for the sake of the kingdom of heaven, I would have waited more happily for your embraces.

But I, poor fool, churned and foamed like a troubled sea, following the rushing of my own tide. Forgetting you, I went beyond all your limits. Yet I didn't escape your strong punishments! What mortal can? But you were always with me, mercifully severe, and you sprinkled all my unlawful pleasures with a most bitter disgust, so that I would search for pleasures free from anxiety. But I couldn't discover where to find such pleasures, except in you, Lord. You teach by sorrow, you wound us in order to heal, and you kill us so that we may not die separated from you.

Where was I, and how far was I exiled from the delights of your house in that sixteenth year of my mortal life, when the madness of lust (to which human shamelessness gives license, although it's forbidden by your Law) held complete sway over me and I surrendered myself to it entirely? Meanwhile, my friends took no care to save me from ruin by encouraging me to get married. Their only concern was that I should learn to speak excellently and become a persuasive orator.

 Sexual lust was a major temptation for Augustine, and here he admits to giving into that temptation at sixteen.

That year my studies were stopped for a time, after my return from Madaura (a neighboring town where I had been sent to learn grammar and rhetoric). My father then provided expenses for a journey to Carthage—out of his determination rather than his means, for he was only a poor freeman [that is, not a slave but still of low social standing] of Tagaste.

Who am I writing this to? Not to you, my God, but in your presence, to my fellow men and women, or at least to that small portion of them who may see these writings of mine. And for what purpose? So that whoever reads this may consider out of what depths we are to cry to you.

Here he's giving some hints as to why he's writing these confessions.

For what comes nearer to your ears than a confessing heart and a life of faith? Who didn't praise my father for the fact that he went beyond his ability and means to furnish his son with everything he needed for a long journey for the sake of his education? Many far abler citizens did no such thing for their children. But yet this same father had no concern as to how I grew toward you, or how morally pure in thought and conduct I was, as long as I was skillful in speech. It didn't matter how fruitless I might have been to your cultivation of my heart, which is your field, God, the only true and good Lord.

But while in my sixteenth year, I lived with my parents, leaving all schools for a while. A season of inactivity and stagnation was caused by my parents' financial circumstances. During that time the briers of unclean desire grew profusely over my head, and there was no hand to root them out. When my father saw me at the baths, realizing that I was becoming a man and was endued with a restless youthfulness, he, as if already anticipating his future grandchildren, gleefully told my mother about it, rejoicing in the intoxication of the senses in which the world forgets its Creator and falls in love with the creature instead of you—the intoxication of the invisible wind of a perverse and downward-tending will that stoops to the most degrading of things.

Augustine's mother, Monica, was a faithful and devout Christian. His father, Patricius, had been a pagan (practicing the religion of the traditional Roman gods), but he had recently become a catechumen, meaning he was in a stage leading up to Christian baptism.

But in my mother's heart you had already begun your temple, and the initial stage of your holy dwelling place. My father, on the other hand, was as yet only a catechumen, and even that only recently. She was jolted then with a holy fear and trembling, and though I wasn't yet baptized, she was afraid of the crooked ways in which people walk who turn their backs to you rather than their faces.

I was miserable! Do I dare say that you held your tongue, my God, while I strayed farther from you? Did you then indeed hold your tongue to me? And whose but yours were the words that you sang in my ears through my mother, your faithful servant? But none of them sank into my heart to make me perform them. For she despised these erratic wanderings, and I remember she warned me in private with great concern and anxiousness not to enter into sexual liaisons, but especially never to defile another man's wife.

To me these seemed like foolish words, coming as they were from a woman, which I would be embarrassed to obey. But they were yours, and I didn't know it. I thought you were silent and that she was the one who was speaking. Yet all the time through her you were speaking to me words that I despised, I who am "your servant, as was my mother before me" (Psalm 115:16). But I didn't know it.

I ran at breakneck speed with such blindness that among my peers I was ashamed to be less shameless than they were when I heard them boast of their disgraceful acts. The greater the degradation, the greater was their boast. And I took pleasure both in the deed and in the praise. What is worthy of blame but degrading, immoral acts or habits? But I made myself out to be even worse than I was so that I might not be disapproved of. When I hadn't sinned in some way like the others who were more abandoned in their sin, I would say that I had done what I hadn't done so that I wouldn't seem contemptible to them in my relative innocence, or thought less of for being somewhat purer in my thoughts and conduct.

These were the companions with whom I walked the streets of Babylon, and wallowed in its filthy mud, as if it were a bed of spices and precious ointments!

 "Walking the streets of Babylon" is Augustine's way of saying that he had seen too much Mardi Gras. Ancient Babylon, told of in the Old Testament book of Daniel, was the capital of a kingdom that once included the lands of modern-day Iraq, Iran, and Israel. Daniel speaks of the city and the kingdom as becoming corrupted by "wine" and "fornication."

And so that I might be joined more firmly to the very root of sin, my invisible enemy stomped me down and seduced me, and at that time I was easy to seduce!

But although my mother had now "fled from Babylon" (Jeremiah 51:6), at least out of its center, she continued more slowly when she reached its outskirts. She advised me to be morally pure in my thoughts and conduct, but paid no attention to what her husband had told her about me, in order to restrain within the bounds of married love what she felt to be now destructive and dangerous for the future (if it couldn't be pared away completely).

My mother didn't pay attention to this, because she was afraid that a wife might prove a barrier and hindrance to my hopes—not the hopes of the world to come, which she had in you, but the hopes of education, which both my parents were too anxious for me to acquire—my father because he had little or no thought of you and only excessively proud thoughts for me, and my mother because she thought that those usual courses of learning would not only not be a drawback, but even of some help towards my attaining you. I'm guessing about this, recalling the best I can the respective attitudes of my parents.

The restraints, meanwhile, were loosened toward me beyond all proper limits. I was allowed to spend my time in sports, yes, even in indulging in sensual pleasures, in doing whatever I wanted. And in all this, darkness was coming between me and the brightness of your truth, my God; "the evil conceits of my mind knew no limits" (Psalm 73:7).

Stealing is punished by your law, Lord, and the law written on our hearts that gross immorality itself can't blot out. For what thief can stand another thief? Not even a rich thief will tolerate one who steals through need. Yet I had a desire to steal, and did so, compelled not by hunger or poverty, but through boredom of doing the right thing and lust for gross immorality. For I stole a small amount of something of which I had enough and much better.

 This begins a long and famous section in which Augustine admits to stealing some pears from an orchard as a teenager. He goes on at some length, trying to discover what led him to commit this sin (and, truth be told, some people think he's being a little too hard on himself here!).

I didn't care to enjoy what I stole, but rather to enjoy the act of stealing and the sin itself. There was a pear tree near our vineyard, heavily loaded with fruit that lacked both color and flavor to tempt us. Some of us worthless young boys went late one night to shake the tree and steal its pears, having prolonged our games in the streets till then, as our disgraceful habit was. We took huge loads of these pears, not to eat ourselves, but to throw to the hogs—all we did was taste them. And it pleased us all the more to do this because we were doing something forbidden.

Observe my heart, God, observe my heart, which you had pity on when it was in the bottomless pit. Let this heart of mine tell you what it was trying to discover there, that I would be evil for nothing, and that my sin would have no cause but the sin itself. It was foul and I loved it; that is, I loved my own perishing. I loved my own wrongdoing—not the thing for which I committed the wrong, but the very act of doing the wrong thing. Foul soul, leaving a place of safety with you, God, and leaping down into destruction, endeavoring to gain nothing through shame but the shame itself!

There is attractiveness in all beautiful bodies, in gold and silver and all things. Bodily contact has its own powerful influence, and each other sense has its proper purpose when used in moderation. Worldly honor also has its glory, as have the power of command and strength to overcome. But from these also comes the desire for revenge. Yet, to acquire all these, we must not depart from you, Lord, or violate your law.

The life we live here has its own attractiveness through a certain measure of beauty of its own and its correspondence with all beautiful things here below. Human friendship is endeared with a sweet tie in a unity formed of many souls. On account of this, sin is committed when through an inordinate appetite for these goods of the lowest order, we forsake the better and higher ones—you yourself, our Lord God, your truth, and your law. For these lower things have their delights, but not like my

God, who made all things. "The righteous will rejoice in the LORD . . . all the upright in heart will glory in him" (Psalm 64:10).

So when we ask why a crime was done, we assume that it could have been done only through some desire of obtaining some of those things that we call lesser goods, or out of fear of losing them. Truly they are beautiful and attractive, even though compared with those higher and blessed goods they're contemptible and coarse. A man has murdered another. Why? He envied his wife or his estate. Or a person would rob for his own livelihood, or the fear of losing something of the kind through the action of the one he was robbing; or, having been wronged, he started a fire out of revenge. Would anyone commit murder for no cause at all, simply delighting in murdering? Who would believe it?

As for that furious and savage man Catiline, of whom it's said that he was evil and cruel without cause, a cause is nevertheless discovered. "I did it," he says, "to keep my hand and heart from becoming inactive."

 Remember that Augustine was a good student of ancient history. He knew about Catiline from his reading of Sallust, an author of grammar classics from the curriculum at that time. Well, Catiline was a Roman who died in 62 BC. Sallust portrays him as a villain and a conspirator, who led a gang of similar young men doing terrible things because he was "essentially evil."

And for what purpose? So that, when he had taken the city through his practice of crimes, he might gain honor, empire, riches, and be freed from fear of the laws that he was afraid of because he know his own viciousness; and so that he and his family might be freed from the possibility of being in need. So, even Catiline himself didn't love his own vicious deeds, but something else, and to obtain these he became wicked.

Then what did I, miserable as I was in that sixteenth year of my life, love so much about stealing, that deed of darkness? Stealing, you weren't beautiful; you were stealing. But are you anything at all, that I should argue with you in this way? The pears that we stole were pleasing to look at, because they were your creation, you who are the most pleasing of all, Creator of all, God of goodness, God, the highest Good and my true Good. Those pears were pleasant to the sight, but my soul didn't want them. I had ample quantities better than those. I picked them only in order to steal. And when I had stolen them I threw them away. My only gratification was my own sin that I was pleased to enjoy. Because if any of those pears entered my mouth, what sweetened their taste was sin.

Now I ask, Lord my God, what was it in that stealing that delighted me? It has no beauty in it— I mean not such beauty as there is in justice and wisdom; or such as is in the mind, the memory, and the vital life of humanity; or yet what is in the stars, glorious and beautiful in their orbits; or the earth or sea, full of fresh offspring constantly taking the place of what is being used up. No, it doesn't even have that false and dark beauty that belongs generally to deceptive immoral acts.

It's pride that imitates a high position, but you alone are God, exalted above all. And what does ambition endeavor to gain except honor and glory? But you alone are to be honored above all and are glorious for ever.

By cruelty the powerful want to be feared, but no one is to be feared but God alone, out of whose power nothing can be wrenched or snatched away—when, where, or by whom?

The come-ons of the lustful person want to be thought of as love, but nothing is so enticing as your love. We can love nothing more healthfully than your truth, bright and beautiful above all.

Curiosity pretends to be a right desire for knowledge, but you're the One who understands all things supremely. Yes, even ignorance and foolishness cloak themselves under the name of simplicity and harmlessness, but nothing is more singular than you, and what is more harmless than you, since it's their own works that bring harm to sinners?

Yes, slothfulness seems to long for rest, but what rest is there, but in the Lord? Luxuriousness parades as plenty and abundance, but you're the fullness and never-failing abundance of pleasures that are incorruptible. Wastefulness presents a semblance of liberality, but you're the most overflowing Giver of all good. Covetousness—resentful desire for something that belongs to someone else—wants to possess many things, but you're the Possessor of all things.

Envy wrangles for first place, but who can be ahead of you? Anger seeks revenge; who can avenge justly but you? Fear jumps with alarm at the unexpected and sudden event that threatens things we love, and is cautious about their security, but who can separate those you love from you? Grief pines away for the lost delight of its desires, and doesn't want to be deprived of anything more than you can be.

In these ways the soul commits "fornication"—the moral equivalent of sexual liaisons—when we turn from you, searching without you for what we can't find to be pure and unblemished until we return to you. Therefore all who separate themselves far from you and raise themselves up against you, are patterning themselves after you. But even by imitating you in these ways, they acknowledge that you're the Creator of all nature, and that there's no place where they can run away and hide from you completely.

Why do we commit wrongs (like stealing pears)? Sometimes just for the thrill, for Augustine didn't actually need the pears.

What, then, did I love in that stealing, and how did I even corruptly and perversely pattern myself after my Lord? Did I wish to break your law by a kind of trick because I couldn't do it by a strong hand? While I was no better than a slave, did I fake a false liberty by doing without punishment what I couldn't do without sin, in a shadowy imitation of your unlimited power? Observe this slave of yours, running away from his Lord, and laying hold on a shadow! What rottenness! What monstrosity of life and depth of death! Could I like what was unlawful only because it was unlawful?

"What shall I return to the Lord?" (Psalm 116:12), seeing that while my memory recalls these things, my soul isn't appalled at them? I will love you, Lord, and thank you, and confess your name, because you've forgiven me for these wicked and monstrous deeds of mine, and have melted away my sins as if they were ice. To your grace I turn over whatever sins I haven't committed; for what might I not have done, who even loved a sin for its own sake? Yes, I confess that all has been forgiven me, both the evils I did commit by my own willfulness and those that, by your help, I didn't commit.

What kind of person is it, who, reflecting on their own weakness, dares to credit their moral purity and innocence to their own strength, so that they should love you less, as if they needed your mercy less, the mercy by which you forgive the sins of those who turn to you? To those people who have been called by you, have followed your voice and avoided those things that they find me remembering and confessing concerning myself, let me say this: Don't despise me. Sick as I was, I was healed by the same physician whose aid is the reason you weren't sick at all, or rather you were less sick. Instead, I say, love God as much as I do, yes, all the more, since you see that I've been rescued from such deep destruction of sin by the one who preserves you from a similar destruction.

And what return did I get from those things that, when I remember them, cause me to be ashamed—above all the stealing that I loved just for the sake of stealing. Since the stealing itself was nothing, I, who loved it, was all the more miserable! I wouldn't have done it alone. Such as I remember myself to have been then, I would never have done it alone. So what I loved in it was the companionship of my accomplices. So, did I love something else besides the stealing? No, I didn't love anything else; for that circumstance of having accomplices was also nothing.

Who can teach me the truth except the One who enlightens my heart and uncovers its dark corners? What is it that has come to mind to inquire about, discuss, and consider? For if I had loved the pears I stole and wished to enjoy them, I could have done it alone. Merely committing the stealing might have given enough pleasure to satisfy me. I wouldn't have needed to stir the itching of my desires by the incentive of having partners in evil. But since my pleasure wasn't in those pears, but in the offense itself, it needed the fellowship of the company of fellow-sinners.

Ultimately, all sin is rooted in pride—the desire to be like God.

What was this pleasure, then? Surely it was shameful, and I'm in anguished distress that I had it! But yet, what was it? "Who can discern their own errors?" (Psalm 19:12). It was a sport that tickled our hearts at the thought that we were deceiving those who would have vehemently disapproved of it.

Yet again, why was my delight such that I didn't do it alone? Because no one ordinarily laughs alone? Ordinarily no one does, though laughter sometimes overcomes us when no one else is with us, if something preposterous presents itself to our senses or mind. But I wouldn't have done this alone. Alone I could never, never have done it. Observe, my God, before you, the vivid remembrance of my soul! Alone, I would never have committed that theft. For what I stole didn't please me.

Friendship, you're too unfriendly! You mysterious seducer of the soul! Out of amusement and unjustifiable recklessness grew the desire to do harm to others, without wanting our own gain or revenge. But when somebody says, "Let's go, let's do it," we're ashamed not to be shameless.

Who can unravel that twisted and tangled knottiness of my soul? It's foul. I hate to think of it or look at it. But I long for you, my God, you who are righteousness and innocence, fair and beautiful to all pure eyes, and a satisfaction that never deceives. With you is complete rest and untroubled life.

Whoever enters into you, enters into the joy of the Lord, and will have no fear, and will do excellently in the most Excellent One. I strayed far from you in those days of my youth, and wandered too far away from you, my God, my Support and Buttress, and I became to myself a barren land.

At the end of a long and somewhat harsh chapter, Augustine ends with good news: no matter how troubled and barren one becomes through one's own sin, God is always there, waiting to grant us perfect rest, healing, and wholeness.

Chapter Three

From Ages Sixteen to Eighteen

■ came to Carthage, where a cauldron of unholy loves bubbled up all around me. I didn't yet love, but I longed to love, and out of a deep-seated lack I hated myself for the fact that I wasn't lacking. I looked around for something to love, in love with the idea of loving, despising a safe way without snares. For my soul was starving for that inward food, yourself, my God, though that severe hunger caused me no hunger. I had no appetite for incorruptible food, not because I was filled with it, but because the emptier I was, the more I detested it. For this reason my soul was sick and full of ulcers, miserably craving to be excited by the touch of feeling creatures. Yet, if they hadn't had souls, they wouldn't have been objects of love.

To love and be loved was sweet to me, and all the more when I succeeded in enjoying the person I loved. So I polluted the waters of friendship with my unclean appetite, and I dimmed its brightness with the hell of lustfulness. Foul and dishonorable as I was, I wanted, through my great vanity, to be elegant and courtly. I fell headlong then into the love in which I longed to be trapped. My God, my mercy, with how much bitterness did you, out of your great goodness, sprinkle me as a result of that sweetness! For I was loved by another, and we secretly formed a bond of pleasure. Therefore I was firmly tied up in a completely happy and contented manner with sorrow-bringing ties, so that I might be tortured with the burning rods of jealousy, suspicions, fears, anger, and quarrels.

Stage plays also carried me away, full of representations of my miseries, fuel to my fire. Why is it that we like to be made sad by observing grief-filled and tragic scenes that we would by no means want to suffer? Yet we wish as spectators to feel sorrow at them, and this very sorrow is our pleasure. What is this but wretched madness? Those who are affected with these actions are the ones who are most plagued with the actual emotions. When we suffer personally, it's considered misery; when we sympathize with another person who's suffering, it's called mercy. But what sort of compassion is that for fictitious and pretended sufferings? The hearers aren't called on to relieve such suffering, but only to grieve. And the more they grieve, the more they applaud the actor of these fictions. If the calamities of those characters (whether of ancient times, or mere fictitious ones) are portrayed in such a way that the spectators aren't moved to tears, they go away disappointed and critical. But if they're moved to grief, they sit it out attentively and weep for joy.

Do people, then, also love sorrow? Surely all people desire joy. Surely no one likes to be miserable, but is pleased to be merciful. But is it because mercy can't be without sorrow that people love sorrow? This also springs from the vein of friendship. But where does that vein go? To where does it flow?

Here Augustine is bemoaning the joy he took in the theater, which, in his day, most often took the form of a Greek tragedy. He wonders why he tried to find entertainment in the misery of others.

Why does the vein of friendship run into that torrent of dark, sticky tar, bubbling forth those monstrous tides of loathsome lustfulness into which it's deliberately changed and transformed, precipitated and corrupted from its heavenly clearness by its own will?

Shall we put away mercy then? By no means! Rather, let's be content to sometimes love grief. But beware of uncleanness, my soul, under the protection of my God, the God of our fathers, who is to be praised and exalted above all forever. Beware of uncleanness!

I don't take myself to be without pity; but then in the theaters I sympathized with lovers when they sinfully enjoyed one another, although this was done fictitiously in the play. And when they lost one another, as if pitying them I grieved with them, yet had my delight in both. But nowadays I feel much more pity for the person who is pleased about their wickedness than for the one who is thought to endure hardship by missing some insidious pleasure and the loss of some miserable happiness. This is surely the truer mercy, but in it grief doesn't delight us. Although they grieve for a person in misery, people who are genuinely compassionate would rather there were nothing to grieve for. Some sorrow may then be allowed, but no sorrow should be loved. Consequently, Lord God, you who love souls far more purely than we, are more righteously compassionate on them, and yet you're not wounded with any kind of sorrow. But who is sufficient for these things?

But I, miserable one, in those days loved to grieve and searched for things to grieve at; the acting that pleased me best and attracted me most powerfully was the one that drew tears from me. And what wonder was it, that an unhappy sheep, straying from your flock, restless under your care, should become infected with a foul disease? This was my love of griefs—not the kind that would probe me too deeply, because I didn't love to suffer the things that I was looking at. I loved the kind of grief that when I heard its fictions, would scratch the surface lightly. But once that surface was scratched, like nails full of venom, there followed burning, swelling, putrefaction, and horrible corruption. Such was my life! But was it really a life, my God?

Your faithful mercy hovered over me. With grievous wicked behavior I wasted myself, following an unholy curiosity, so that, having forsaken you, it might bring me to the treacherous abyss and to the beguiling service of devils to whom I sacrificed my evil actions. In all these things you punished me severely! I even dared, while your solemnities were celebrated within the walls of your Church, to see and to conclude a business sufficient to procure me the fruits of death. For this you afflicted me with grievous punishments, but nothing in comparison with my fault, you who are my exceeding mercy, my God, my refuge from those terrible hurts! Among them I wandered with stiff-necked presumption, straying farther from you, loving my own ways and not yours, loving an aimless freedom.

Those studies, too, that were considered commendable were directed at excelling in the courts of law. The craftier I was, the greater would be the praise. Such is the blindness of people, that they glory even in their own blindness. And now I was head of my class in the School of Rhetoric. I was proud and pleased at this and was inflated with arrogance, though (Lord, you know) I was far quieter and altogether removed from the undermining of those "underminers" with whom I lived, whose stupid and devilish name was held to be the very badge of gallantry.

Although Augustine was the equivalent of the class president of his school, he still hung out with an unsavory crowd—basically, they were the school bullies.

I felt ashamed that I was ashamed not to be just what they were. I lived with them and was sometimes delighted with their friendship, but I was always revolted by their acts, that is, their "underminings," with which they insolently attacked the modesty of strangers, disturbing others by pointless jeering, gratifying their devilish glee by it. Nothing can be more like the very actions of devils than these. What then could they be more truly called than "underminers," undermined and totally perverted as they were themselves in the first place by the deceiving spirits who derided and seduced them, and then delighting themselves in jeering at and deceiving others?

Among companions such as these, at that unstable period of my life, I studied books of eloquence in which I wanted to be outstanding, from a damnable and boastful ambition, a delight in human vanity.

Cicero lived from 106–43 BC, and he was considered the greatest Roman orator of all time. He was also a politician and a philosopher. Hortensius *was a book he wrote in praise of philosophy, arguing that only through the beauty of philosophy can a human being rise above bodily temptations and be more fully enlightened. We only have fragment of* Hortensius *today.*

In the ordinary course of study, I fell upon a certain book of Cicero, whose language almost everyone admires, though not his heart. This book of his contains an urgent appeal to philosophy, and is called *Hortensius*. But this book, in truth, changed my affections and turned my prayers to you, Lord. It made me have other purposes and other desires. Every vain and useless hope suddenly became worthless to me, and I yearned with incredible warmth of heart for immortality of wisdom, and (like the prodigal son, see Luke 15:18) began to arise, so that I might return to you. For it wasn't to sharpen my tongue that I studied that book (which was what I seemed to be buying with my mother's allowances in my nineteenth year, my father having died two years earlier), nor did it persuade me by its style, but by its very subject matter.

How eager I was then, my God, how eager to rise above earthly things to you! But I didn't know what you would do with me, for with you is wisdom. In Greek the love of wisdom is called "philosophy," and it was this love with which that book stirred me.

There are some who seduce others through philosophy, under a great, alluring, and honorable name, coloring and disguising their own errors. And almost all those who in Cicero's age and before him were seducers of this sort, are set forth and disapproved of in that book. There also is made plain that excellent advice of your Spirit, by your good and devout servant [the apostle Paul], "See to it that no one takes you captive through hollow and deceptive philosophy, which depends on human tradition and the elemental spiritual forces of this world rather than on Christ. For in Christ all the fullness of the Deity lives in bodily form" (Colossians 2:8-9).

At that time, you know, you who are the Light of my heart, I knew nothing about apostolic Scripture. Therefore I was delighted with that urgent appeal only in that I was strongly roused, kindled, and stirred to love, to seek, to obtain, hold, and embrace not this or that sect, but wisdom itself—whatever it might be. And the one thing that checked me in my new enthusiasm was that the name of Christ wasn't in it. For this name, according to your mercy, Lord, this name of my Savior, your Son, my tender heart had devoutly drunk in even with my mother's milk and had deeply treasured. So whatever omitted that name, even though it might be ever so scholarly, polished, and true, never took complete hold on me.

I resolved, then, to direct my mind in the Holy Scriptures, so that I might learn what they contained. And I saw something that the proud don't understand and that hasn't been revealed to the ignorant, something that is humble as you approach it, sublime as you advance in it, and veiled in mysteries. I wasn't one of those who could enter into it or submit myself to follow its steps.

Reading Cicero led Augustine to read the Bible, and here he writes about the difference between the two.

For when I turned to those Scriptures I didn't feel as I do when I speak now. They appeared to me unworthy to be compared to the dignity of Cicero, because my inflated pride shrank from their humble style, and my sharp mind couldn't pierce their inner meaning. Yet they were the kind of thing that would grow in a beginner—only I considered it beneath me to be a beginner. Swollen with pride, I looked on myself as a great person.

Then I fell in with a group of very worldly, talkative, and proud persons, in whose mouths were the snares of the devil, lined with a mixture of the syllables of your name and of our Lord Jesus Christ, and of the Holy Spirit, the Paraclete, our Comforter. These names were always in their mouths, but only in sound and the noise of the tongue, for their heart was empty of truth. They cried out "Truth! Truth!" and spoke of it a great deal to me, yet it wasn't in them. They spoke falsehood, not only of you, who in truth are Truth, but also of the elements of this world, your creation.

I ought to have ignored philosophers, even when they spoke the truth concerning those elements, out of love for you, Father, you who are supreme Good, the Beauty of all beautiful things. Truth! How inwardly did the marrow of my soul pant after you even then, when they frequently and in many ways, in numerous and lengthy books, echoed your name to me, even though it was only an echo! And these were the dishes that they served to me, hungering as I was for you: the sun and moon. These are beautiful works of yours, but they're still your works, not yourself, not even your first works. For your spiritual works came before these physical ones, heavenly and shining though they may be.

But I was hungry and thirsty, not even for those first works, but for you yourself, the Truth, "who does not change like shifting shadows" (James 1:17). Yet they still set glittering fantasies before me in those dishes.

It would be better to love the sun itself, which is at least real to our sight, than the illusions that deceive our minds through our eyes. Yet because I supposed them to be you, I fed on them. It wasn't an eager feeding, because you didn't taste to me as you are. For you weren't present in those empty fictions, and I wasn't nourished by them, but exhausted instead. Food in our dreams looks very much like our real food, but sleepers aren't nourished by it, because they're asleep. And those fantasies weren't in any way like you, as you've since revealed yourself to me, for those were all material fantasies, false bodies.

The true bodies, celestial or earthly, that we observe with our physical eyes are far more true. The animals and birds can see them as well as we can, and they're far more certain than when we imagine them. But we even imagine them more accurately than we conjecture other vast and infinite bodies that have no existence at all. Those were the empty pods on which I was fed. In truth, however, I was still hungry.

But you, my soul's Love, for whom I faint with longing that I might gain strength—you're not those visible bodies, even though they're in heaven, and you aren't the invisible ones, either. For you created those things, and you can create nobler things than they are. How far then are you from those fantasies of mine, fantasies of bodies that don't even exist! The images of bodies that do exist are far more real, and even more real are the bodies themselves—yet they aren't you. No, you're not even the soul that's the life of bodies. Better, then, and more certain is the soul of the bodies than the bodies themselves. But you're the Life of the soul, having life in yourself. And you never change, you who are the Life of my soul!

Where then were you to me in that period of my life, and how far were you from me? I was straying very far from you, kept (like the prodigal son, see Luke 15:16) from the very pods that serve as food for pigs, even though I was feeding pods to the pigs. For how much better are the fables of poets and grammarians than these traps!

Verses, poems and "Medea flying" are surely of more value than the five elements, depicted in various ways, answering to "five caves of darkness,"

 In Greek mythology, Medea flies around the universe in a chariot, sometimes in order to flee trouble and return to her grandfather, Helios, the Sun. Augustine studied all of

that thoroughly in school. He contrasts it to five elements and five caves of darkness which are references to the elaborate Manichean mythology that he has just gotten himself out of.

None of these things exist, yet they kill the believer. I can turn verses and poems into true food, and though I sang "Medea flying," I didn't really believe it. Even though I heard people sing about it, I had no faith in it—but those things I did believe.

I was miserable! My God, I confess it to you, who had mercy on me, whom I didn't yet confess, that laboring and in turmoil through lack of truth, I searched for you. And this was not according to the understanding of the mind in which you willed that I should surpass the animals, but according to the sense of the flesh! You were more inward to me than my most inward part, and higher than my highest.

I came upon that bold and shameless woman, who is simple and knows nothing, who sits at the door in Solomon's allegory, saying, "Stolen water is sweet; food eaten in secret is delicious!" (Proverbs 9:17). She seduced me because she found my soul outside her gates, lingering in what was outward and material, and carefully reflecting on such food as I had absorbed in that manner.

Other than this, I didn't know what reality truly was. I was persuaded, through a sharp mind, to agree with foolish deceivers when they asked me, "Where does evil come from?"

Here Augustine is starting to write about his early philosophical problems with the Bible. Being a strong follower of Plato's philosophy, he thought of God as a great eternal mind, and he couldn't conceive of the very earthy and personal God in the Old and New Testaments.

"Is God limited by a bodily shape, and does he have hair and nails?" "Are we to consider righteous those who had many wives at once, and killed many people, and sacrificed living animals?" In my ignorance, I was troubled at these questions, and departed from the truth even though I was making headway towards it. I didn't know that evil was nothing but an absence of good, until at last a thing completely ceases to be.

How could I see this, when my eyes could see only physical bodies and my mind only fantasies? I didn't know that God is a Spirit, not a being who has parts extended in length and breadth, or whose being has bulk. For every bulk is less in part than in its whole, and if it's infinite, it must be less than the space in which it's contained. So it can't be wholly everywhere, as a Spirit is, as God is. And I had no idea what in us might be God, and what might rightly in Scripture be said to be "in God's image" (Genesis 1:27).

I also didn't know the true inward righteousness that doesn't judge according to custom, but out of the most perfect law of God Almighty. For though the manners of places and times are adapted to those times and places, that perfect law in itself is always the same everywhere, not one thing in one place and another in another. According to this, Abraham, Isaac, Jacob, Moses, and David were righteous, as well as all those who were commended by the mouth of God. But they were judged to be unrighteous by foolish people who measured by their own petty standards the manners of the whole human race.

It's as if a soldier, one who is ignorant of what armor is suitable for various parts of the body, were to cover his head with armor designed for the legs, and tried to put a helmet on his feet, complaining that they didn't fit. Or, as if on a day when business is publicly stopped in the afternoon, one were angry at not being allowed to keep his shop open because it was lawful for him to be open in the morning.

 He's using an analogy of a soldier dressing incorrectly to point out that he was inappropriately trying to get the Old Testament to conform to his standards of Greek philosophy. That is, he wanted the Bible's understanding of "righteousness" to match Plato's version of "righteousness."

Or when he sees some servant pick up something in his hand that his butler isn't allowed to touch, or something is done outdoors that's forbidden in the dining room, he should be angry that in one house and one family, the same thing isn't allowed everywhere and to everybody.

It's exactly the same with those who can't endure to hear that something was lawful to the righteous in other ages that isn't lawful now, or that God, for certain historical reasons, commanded some people to do one thing, and some another, while both of them obeyed the same justice. Yet they see in one person, one day, and one house, different things are suitable for different members and a thing that was formerly lawful, after a certain time became unlawful—permitted or commanded in one corner, but rightly forbidden and punished in another.

Is justice therefore variable and changeable? No, but the times over which it rules aren't all alike, because they're historical. Human beings, whose days are few upon the earth, can't harmonize by their own perceptions the causes of former ages and other nations, with which they haven't had any experience, with those with which they do have experience. When it concerns a single body, day, or family, they easily see what is fitting for each member, season, part, or person. They take exception to what was formerly done, but readily submit to the manners of the present.

These things I didn't know or observe then. They were in my plain sight all the time, but I didn't see them. I wrote poems in which I couldn't place every unit of poetic meter everywhere, but one way in one meter, and a different way in another. Even in the same meter, the same unit of stressed and unstressed syllables couldn't be used everywhere. Yet the art itself, by which I composed, didn't have different principles for these different cases, but included them all in one.

I still didn't see how that righteousness, which good and holy people obeyed, more excellently and sublimely included in one single thing all those things that God commanded, and never varied. In varying times it didn't prescribe everything at once, but apportioned and required what was proper for the circumstances. In my blindness, I blamed the patriarchs, not only where they made use of things that God commanded and inspired them to do, but also for predicting things to come as God revealed them.

Can it ever be wrong to love God with all one's heart, soul, and mind, and to love one's neighbor as one's self? Therefore, the foul offenses that are against nature are everywhere and at all times detested and punished, such as were those of the people of Sodom (see Genesis 13:13). Even if all nations were to commit to this, they would all stand guilty of the same crime by the law of God, which didn't make human beings in order for them to abuse one another in that way. For even the fellowship that should exist between God and us is violated, when that same nature of which he is Author, is polluted by the perversity of lust.

But those offenses that are contrary to human customs are to be avoided according to what prevails in different customs, so that a thing agreed on and confirmed by the custom or law of any city or nation may not be violated at the lawless pleasure of anyone, by citizen or stranger. For any part that isn't consistent with the whole is offensive.

But when God commands anything to be done contrary to the customs or laws of any people, though they had never done it before, it must be done; and if it has been dropped for a time, it must be restored; and if it was never established, it must be established. For if it's lawful for a king, in the country over which he reigns, to command what he himself or anyone before him had never previously commanded, and if it isn't against the common welfare of the state to obey him (indeed it would be against the common welfare if he weren't obeyed, for it's a general agreement of human society that rulers are to be obeyed), how much more unhesitatingly ought we to obey God in all he commands, he who is the Ruler of all his creatures! For as among the authorities of human society the greater authority is obeyed above the lesser one, so must God be obeyed above all.

In some sins there is a real will to harm another, as in acts of violence (either by harsh words or physical injury). In either case the deed is done either for the sake of revenge (as one enemy against another), or to gain some desired thing that belongs to another (as the robber to the traveler); or to avoid some evil (as when one person is afraid of another); or through envy (as when a less fortunate person attacks a more prosperous one, or when a prospering one attacks another who is equal to him, whose equality he's afraid of or resents); or for mere pleasure in another's pain (as in the case of spectators of gladiators, or of those who mock others or treat them with contempt).

These are the chief sins that spring from the lust of the flesh, of the eye, and of power, either singly, or two of them combined, or all of them together. This is the way people live in contradiction to the Three [commandments that give us duty to you] and Seven [commandments that give us duty to others], that "ten-stringed lyre" (Psalm 92:3), your Ten Commandments, God most high and most sweet.

But what foul offenses can there be against you, who can't be defiled? What acts of violence can there be against you who can't be harmed? You avenge what human beings perpetrate against themselves, for when they sin against you, they sin against their own souls, and gross immorality lies to itself, by corrupting and perverting their nature that you created and ordained. Or they sin by an excessive use of things that are permitted or in a burning desire for things that are forbidden to any use that's against nature; or when they're found guilty, raging with heart and tongue against you, kicking against the goads (as Saul describes himself in Acts 26:14). Or they sin by breaking through the restraints of human society, boldly rejoicing in private combinations or divisions, depending on whether they see an object to be gained or want to take revenge for some offense. These things are done whenever people forsake you, who are the Fountain of Life, the only true Creator and Ruler of the universe, and whenever self-willed pride selects and loves any false thing.

So, by a humble devotion and reverence we return to you. Then you cleanse us from our evil habits, you're merciful toward the sins of those who confess to you, you hear the groans of the prisoners (Psalm 102:20), and you release us from the chains that we forged for ourselves, if we don't lift up the horns of a counterfeit liberty against you, losing everything by craving more, by loving our own private good more than you, who are the Good of all.

Amid all these offenses of evil acts, violence, and gross immorality are the sins of those who are on the whole making progress. These sins are disapproved of by those who judge right and after the rule of perfection, yet the persons themselves are encouraged in the hope of bearing fruit, like the green blade of growing grain.

There are also acts that resemble offenses of infamy or violence that aren't sins, because they don't offend you, our Lord God, nor human society. When, for example, things that are suitable for the time are provided for the use of life, we don't know whether they involve a lust to possess; or when acts are punished by constituted authority for the sake of correction, we don't know whether the punishment involves a lust for causing pain. Many a deed, then, which in our sight is disapproved, is approved by your testimony, and many actions that we praise, you condemn, because the outward appearance of the deed and the mind of the doer, and the unknown circumstance of the moment vary. But when you suddenly command an unusual and unthought-of thing—yes, although you've formerly forbidden it and still at present are hiding the reason for your command, even if it's against the ordinance of some human society, who can doubt that it's to be done? How blessed are those who know your commands! For your servants did all kinds of things, either to exhibit something necessary for that time, or to predict things to come.

Being ignorant of these things, I scoffed at your holy servants and prophets. What did I gain by scoffing at them but to be scoffed at by you, being unknowingly, and little by little, led on to my foolishness, so as to believe that a fig tree wept when the fig was plucked, and the tree from which it was picked, its mother, shed milky tears?

Here he is starting to unravel the strange beliefs of Manicheism, in which he was wrapped at the time, including that it was forbidden to pick fruit because that was considered a form of cannibalism!

This fig, nevertheless, having been picked by someone else (thereby incurring the guilt) some [Manichean] saint was then able to eat it without guilt, and mingling it in his bowels, he would have breathed out angels. Yes, and there would burst forth particles of divinity at every moan or groan in his prayer, which particles of the most high and true God would have remained bound in that fig if they had not been freed by the teeth or belly of some "elect" saint! And I, pathetic one, believed that more mercy was to be shown to the fruits of the earth than to human beings for whom they were created. For if a hungry person who wasn't a Manichean were hungry and asked for a bite, any morsel given to him would appear, so to speak, condemned to capital punishment.

You sent your hand from above and drew out my soul from that profound darkness, because my mother, your faithful one, continued to weep before you on my behalf more than mothers weep over the bodily death of their children. By the faith and spirit that she had from you, she saw that I was dead. You heard her, Lord. You heard her and didn't despise her tears that streamed down and watered the ground under her eyes wherever she prayed. Yes, you heard her!

Where did that dream come from by which you so comforted her that she allowed me to live with her and eat at the same table in her house (something she had begun to deny me, since she loathed and detested the blasphemy of my error)? In her dream she saw herself standing on a certain wooden rule, and a bright young man was coming toward her, cheerful and smiling at her, as she was grieving and overcome with sorrow. He asked her the cause of her grief and tears she shed every day (not that he needed to be instructed, but in order to instruct her), and she answered that she was expressing her grief that I was utterly lost. He encouraged her to rest contented, and told her to look and observe that where she was, there I was as well. When she looked, she saw me standing by her on the same rule. Where could this have come from, but that your ears were inclined to her heart, Almighty Good? You care for every one of us as if you cared for each of us alone, yet you care for everyone together as you care for each one individually!

And it must have come from the same Source, that when she told me about this vision, and I wanted to twist it to mean instead that she shouldn't despair of being one day what I was, she replied without any hesitation, "No! For I wasn't told, 'Where he is there you will be,' but 'Where you are, there he will be.'" I confess to you, Lord, that to the best of my memory (and I have often spoken of this), your answer through my now-awake mother—that she wasn't confused by the plausibility of my false interpretation and saw in a moment what was to be seen, and that I certainly hadn't perceived before she spoke—even then moved me more than the dream itself. It was through that dream that the happiness of that devout woman, to be realized so long after, was foretold in order to alleviate her anxiety.

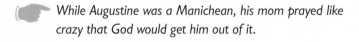 *While Augustine was a Manichean, his mom prayed like crazy that God would get him out of it.*

Almost nine years passed in which I wallowed in the filthy muck of that deep pit and the darkness of falsehood, often trying to climb out of it, but always grievously dashed down. And all this time that morally pure, godly, and sober widow (of the kind that you love), now cheered with hope, yet not relaxing one moment in her weeping and mourning, never ceased at all the hours of her prayers to cry over my case before you. Her "prayers came before you" (Psalm 88:2). Yet you allowed me to be wrapped up and still more wrapped up in that darkness.

Meanwhile, you gave her another answer, which I remember. For I'm skipping a lot of things in order to confess the things that are most important, and I'm skipping over a lot that I don't remember. You granted her another answer by a priest of yours, a certain bishop brought up in your Church and well versed in your Scriptures. She asked him to talk with me, refute my errors, and teach me good things. He was in the habit of doing this when he found persons ready to receive it. He refused— wisely, however, as I afterward came to see, and answered that I was still unteachable, since I was inflated with the novelty of the Manichean heresy, and that I had already confused various inexperienced persons with tricky questions, as my mother had related to him.

"Leave him alone for a while," he said. "Just pray to God for him. All by himself he'll find out by reading what that error is and how great is its lack of reverence for the true God."

At the same time he told her how he himself, when he was only a child, had been turned over to the Manicheans by his mother, and had not only read but even copied out by hand almost all their books. But without any argument or proof from anyone, he had come to see how much that sect ought to be avoided, and avoid it he did. When my mother wouldn't be satisfied with this, but pressed him more urgently with many tears, he agreed to see me and talk with me, a little irritated by her insistence.

"Go your way and God bless you," he said, "for it isn't possible that the son of these tears should perish." She accepted this answer (as she often mentioned in her conversations with me) as if it had been spoken from heaven.

Chapter Four

From Ages Eighteen to Twenty-seven

For a period of nine years, from age eighteen to twenty-seven, I lived seduced and seducing, deceived and deceiving, in various forms of unholy desires: openly, by teaching what they call liberal sciences; secretly, by adhering to a false religion. Here proud, there superstitious, everywhere preoccupied with myself! On the one hand I was striving after the emptiness of popular praise, down even to theatrical applause, poetic prizes and competitions for grassy garlands, the follies of entertainments and untempered lusts. On the other hand, I desired to be cleansed of these defilements by carrying food to those who were called Elect and Holy, out of which, in the laboratories of their stomachs, they should forge for us angels and gods by whom we might be cleansed. I followed these things and practiced them with my friends who were deceived by me and with me.

Let the arrogant make fun of me, those who haven't yet been struck down by you, my God. But I would still in your praise confess my own shame to you. Bear with me, and give me grace, I pray, to go over the wanderings of former years, and to offer to you the sacrifice of thanksgiving. For without you, what am I to myself, but a guide to my own downfall? Or at my best, what am I but an infant suckled on your milk and feeding on you, who are the Food that never perishes? But what sort of person is anyone, since he or she is only a human being? Let the strong and mighty laugh at me. In my need and helplessness I will confess to you.

In those years I taught rhetoric, and driven by an inordinate desire for wealth, I offered the art of speaking for sale. Yet you know, Lord, that I preferred honest students, as honesty goes, and that I taught them tricks, not to be used against the life of the guiltless, but that they might sometimes use them to save the life of the guilty. From afar, God, you saw me stumbling in that slippery path amid much smoke, sending out some sparks of faithfulness that I showed in my guidance of those who "loved delusions and sought false gods" (Psalm 4:2). In truth I was their companion.

In those years I had a mistress, not a wife in lawful marriage, but a woman whom I had met following my willfully perverse passion, as empty of understanding as I was.

Here's the first mention of Augustine's "love," a woman he lived with for thirteen years, but she is never named. Today, she might be thought of as his "common-law" wife.

I remained faithful to her, and experienced for myself what difference there is between the self-restraint of the marriage covenant made for the sake of raising a family and the bargain of a lustful love, where children are born against their parents' will, although, once born, they may compel our love.

I remember also, that when I had decided to enter a contest for a theatrical prize, a fortuneteller asked me what I would give him to win. Detesting and despising such foul mysteries, I answered, "Though the wreath should be made of gold itself, I would not permit a fly to be killed to gain it." For he would have killed a certain living creature to sacrifice, and by that means invite the devils to favor me. I rejected this evil, but not out of a pure love for you, God of my heart. For I didn't know how to love you, not knowing how to conceive of anything beyond a material brightness. And doesn't a person who sighs after such idle fictions commit the moral equivalent of fornication against you, trust in unreality, and feed the wind? I wouldn't have him sacrifice to devils for me, but I was sacrificing to them myself by my superstition. What else is it to feed the wind but to feed the devils, that is, by our wanderings to become their pleasure and mockery?

Those imposters whom they call astrologers, I consulted without qualms of conscience, because they didn't used sacrifices and didn't pray to any spirit to predict the future. Yet true Christian devotion and reverence consistently rejects and condemns them, too. For it's a good thing to confess to you and say, "Have mercy on me, LORD, heal me, for I have sinned against you" (Psalm 41:4), and not to abuse your mercy for a license to sin. Instead, we should remember the Lord's words, "See, you are well again. Stop sinning or something worse may happen to you" (John 5:14).

All this good advice these astrologers do their best to destroy, saying, "The cause of your sin is inevitably determined in heaven," and "Venus did this, or Saturn, or Mars," so that you, indeed, who are flesh and blood and proud corruption, may be blameless, while the Creator and Ordainer of heaven and the stars is to bear the blame. But who is that One but our God, the very Sweetness and Wellspring of righteousness, who "will repay everyone according to what they have done" (Romans 2:6), "who will not despise a broken and contrite heart" (Psalm 51:17)?

In those days there was a wise man who was proconsul, very learned and well known in medicine, who with his own hand put a wreath on my sick head, though not in his capacity as a physician. For this disease only you can cure, you who "oppose the proud but show favor to the humble" (1 Peter 5:5). You spoke to me, even through that old man, to heal my soul.

A "proconsul" was a government official in the Roman Empire, and this one was also a "man of science." The wreath he put on Augustine's sin-sick head was the prize in a poetry contest.

Having become acquainted with him, I hung persistently and fixedly on what he said, for even though he spoke in simple terms, his words were vivid, lively, and earnest. When he gathered from our conversations that I was quite attracted by the books of astrology, with the kindliness of a father he advised me to throw them away, and not to waste any care or attention on these worthless things. He said that he had studied that art in his earlier years, intending to make it his profession. Since he understood Hippocrates' principles of medicine, he could just as easily have understood such a subject as this. Yet he had abandoned it and taken up medicine for one reason only: He found astrology to be utterly false, and as a serious man, he wouldn't earn his living by deceiving people.

"But you," he said, "you have rhetoric to support yourself by, so you follow this by free choice and not by necessity. That's all the more reason to believe me, who labored to acquire it so perfectly that I could make my living by it alone."

When I then demanded to know how it is that many true things could be foretold by astrology, he answered me as best he could that the force of chance, spread through the whole order of things, made it possible. For when one by chance opened the pages of some poet, who sang and thought of something wholly different, a verse oftentimes fell out that was wondrously suited to the present circumstance. It isn't to be wondered at if, out of the soul of human beings, by some higher but unconscious instinct within it, an answer should be given, not by art but by mere chance, that corresponds to the business and actions of the questioner.

Either from him or through him, you conveyed to me and planted in my memory what I would later examine for myself. But at that time neither he nor my dear friend Nebridius, a young man singularly good and morally pure, who laughed at the whole subject of foretelling the future, could persuade me to forsake it. The authority of the authors still influenced me more greatly, and as yet I had found no certain proof, such as I was looking for, by which it might be shown beyond all doubt, that what had been accurately forecast by those consulted was the result of chance rather than the art of stargazers.

In those years when I first began to teach rhetoric in my native town, I had acquired a very dear friend of my own age from association in our studies. Like me, he was in the first opening flower of youth. We had grown up together as children, and we had been both fellow students and playmates. But he wasn't yet my friend as he became later, nor even then as true friendship is. For no friendship can be true unless you are the bond that holds it together, binding it yourself by that love that has been "poured out into our hearts through the Holy Spirit, who has been given to us" (Romans 5:5).

Yet that friendship was too sweet, ripened as it was by the warmth of similar studies; for I had turned Nebridius from the true faith, which he had not soundly and thoroughly taken in as a youth, toward those destructive and superstitious fables that my mother grieved over in me. He now went astray with me in these errors, and my soul couldn't be without him. But you were close on the steps of your fugitives. At once God of vengeance and fountain of mercies, you turn us to yourself by wonderful means. You took that man from this life after scarcely a year of a friendship that had grown sweet to me above all the sweetness of my life.

"Who can fully declare your praise" (Psalm 106:2) that one has felt in himself alone? What did you do then, my God, and how unsearchable are the depths of your judgments! For a long time my friend lay unconscious in a death-sweat, very sick of a fever. With the hope of his recovery being lost, he was baptized without his knowledge. Meanwhile, I paid little regard, presuming that his soul would retain what it had received from me, not what was done to his unconscious body through baptism. But it proved otherwise, for he was received and restored.

Then, as soon as I could speak with him (and I could as soon as he was able, for I never left him, and we hung all too much on each other), I tried to banter with him, thinking that he would joke with me about the baptism that he had received when totally without consciousness or feeling. But he drew back from me, as from an enemy. In a remarkable and unexpected freedom, he told me that if I wanted to continue to be his friend, to refrain from speaking to him in such a way. Completely confounded and amazed, I concealed all my emotions, waiting till he got well and his health got strong enough for me to deal with him as I wished.

But he was removed from my madness so that he might be saved by you for my comfort. A few days later, during my absence, he had a return of the fever, and died.

My heart was utterly darkened by this grief. Whatever I looked at was death. My native country was torture to me, and my father's house a strange unhappiness. Whatever I had shared with my friend became in his absence a frightful torture. My eyes looked for him everywhere in vain. I hated all places because he wasn't in them. Nor could they now say to me, "He will be coming," as they did when he was alive and absent. I became a great puzzle to myself, and asked my soul why it was so sad, and why it troubled me so deeply. But my soul didn't have an answer for me. And if I said "Hope in God," it wouldn't obey me, because that most dear friend, whom it had lost, being a human, was better and more real than the imagined deity it was asked to trust in. Nothing was sweet to me but tears, and they filled the emptiness my friend had left in the affections of my heart.

These things are long past, Lord, and time has healed my wound. May I learn from you, who are the truth? May I hold the ear of my heart close to your mouth, so that you may tell me why tears are sweet to those in sorrow? Have you, although you are present everywhere, cast away our misery far from you? You abide in yourself, while we are tossed about with various trials. And yet, if we didn't weep in your ears, we would have no hope left.

From where, then, comes the sweet fruit gathered from the bitterness of life, from groans, tears, sighs, and laments? Does it sweeten it to hope that you hear? This is true of prayer, for in it there is a longing to approach you. But is it also true in grief for a lost friend, and in the sorrow that then overwhelmed me? For I neither hoped that he would return to life, nor did I ask for this with my tears. I wept and grieved only because I was miserable and had lost my joy. Or is weeping bitter when we have the things we enjoy, only to grow delightful when we lose them?

Why do I speak of these things? For this is no time to ask questions, but to confess to you. I was desolate, as everyone is desolate who is bound by friendship to mortal things. Those who lose them are torn apart, and feel the misery that they were subject to even before they lost them. So it was at that time with me. I wept very bitterly and found my rest in bitterness. So I was miserable, but I held even that life of misery dearer than my friend. For though I would willingly have changed it, yet I was less willing to part with it than with him.

Orestes was a figure from Greek legends, the son of King Agamemnon, who avenged his father's death and then fled with the help of his closest friend, Pylades. The story is actually quite reminiscent of the Old Testament friendship of David and Jonathan.

Yes, I don't know whether I would have parted with it even for him. In the story of Pylades and Orestes, they would gladly have died for one another, since not to live together was to them worse than death. But in me there had grown up some kind of feeling completely contrary to this. At the same time, I hated to live and I was afraid to die. I suppose that the more I loved him, the more I hated and was afraid of death, which as a most cruel enemy, had taken him from me. I imagined that it would make a speedy end of all people, since it had such power over him. This is the way it was with me, as I recall.

See my heart, God. Look deep within me and see, for I well remember it, you who are my Hope, you who cleanse me from the impurity of such affections, directing my eyes toward you, and "releasing my feet from the snare" (Psalm 25:15). I wondered that others who were subject to death should live, since the one whom I loved as if he would never die, was dead. And I wondered yet more that I myself, who was like a second self to him, could still be alive though he was dead. It was well said when someone called his friend "half of my soul," for I felt that my soul and his were one soul in two bodies, and therefore my life was a horror to me, because I wouldn't live if I were cut in half. Therefore, perhaps I was afraid to die because if I died, the person whom I loved so much might die completely.

What madness that doesn't know how to love people as people! How foolish I was then, enduring the lot in life of all people with such impatience! I fretted, sighed, cried, tormented myself, and took neither rest nor advice. I carried about a torn and bleeding soul, tired of being sustained by me, yet I couldn't find anywhere to let it rest. Not in pleasant groves, not in games or music, not in perfumed gardens, not in banqueting, not in the pleasures of the bed and couch—not even in books or poetry did I find rest. All things looked terrible, even the light itself. Whatever wasn't him was nauseating and hateful. Only in groans and tears did I find a little refreshment, and when I gave these up even for a little time, a huge load of misery weighed me down.

My soul should have been lifted up to you, Lord, for you to lighten my burden. I knew it, but was neither willing nor able, for truthfully, when I thought of you, you weren't anything solid or substantial to me. My god wasn't you, yourself, but one of useless imagination and error. If I attempted to lay my load on this god, so that it might rest, it sank into nothingness and came rushing back on me again. I remained an unhappy place to myself, where I couldn't stay and which I couldn't leave. For where could my heart run to get away from my heart? Where could I run from myself? How could I not follow myself? And yet I fled out of my native country, for my eyes would search for him less where they weren't used to seeing him. And so I left Tagaste for Carthage.

Time hurries on. It doesn't roll idly by. Through our senses it works a strange work on the mind. The moments came and went, day by day, and by coming and going introduced other ideas and other remembrances to my mind. Little by little they patched me up again with my old delights, and my sorrow gave way to these. There followed then not other griefs, but the causes for griefs to come. For how could that former grief so easily have reached my inmost soul, except because I had poured out my soul in the dust in loving one who must die, as if he was never going to die?

What restored and refreshed me most was the consolation of other friends whom I loved instead of you. And this was a kind of fable, a drawn-out life by whose adulterous contact my soul, which lay itching in my ears, was being defiled. This fable wouldn't die to me, no matter how often any of my friends might die. There were other things in them that occupied my mind: to talk and joke together, to do each other kindnesses by turn, to read pleasant books together; to play the fool or to be serious together; to disagree at times, as one might do with oneself, and by the infrequency of these differences, seasoning our more frequent agreements. Sometimes we would teach, sometimes we would learn, longing for the absent with impatience, and welcoming their coming with joy. These and other things, proceeding out of the hearts of those that loved and were loved in return, by look, speech, the eyes, and a thousand pleasing gestures, were so much fuel to meld our souls together and out of many to make us one.

This is what we love in friends. We love so much that our conscience condemns us if we don't love one. From this comes our sadness and grief when one dies, the blackness of sorrow, the soaking of the heart in tears, all sweetness turned into bitterness, and with the loss of life of the dying, the "death" of the living.

How blessed is the person who loves you, and their friends in you, and their enemy for your sake. For this is the only person who loses no one dear to them, if all are dear in the One who can't be lost. Who is it but God, the God who made heaven and earth, who fills them, even by filling them with himself, creating them? No one will lose you but the one who leaves you. And in leaving you, where does that person run away to but from your pleasure to your anger? Where can they escape your law, as it is fulfilled in their own punishment? "Your law is true" (Psalm 119:142), and you yourself are truth.

"Restore us, God Almighty; make your face shine on us, that we may be saved" (Psalm 80:7). For no matter where the human soul turns, unless it's toward you, it's riveted to sorrows, yes, even though it's attached to beautiful things. Yet such things would be nothing if they weren't from you. They rise and set: By rising, they begin, so to speak, to be; and they grow toward their completion; and completed, they grow old, and die.

Not all things grow old, but all of them perish. The more quickly they rise, the more rapidly they speed toward not being. This is their law. This much you've allowed them, because they are portions of things that don't exist all at the same time. But by following one another in turn, they make up that universe of which they are parts.

In the same way our speech is completed by separate sounds. It's necessary for one word to pass away when it has sounded its part, so that another may follow it. Out of all these things let my soul praise you, God, creator of all. Don't allow my soul to be fastened to these things with love of them through my physical senses. For they tend toward "not being," tearing the soul with infected, contaminated longings, because it longs to be in them, yet loves to rest in what it loves.

But my soul can't rest in these things; they don't remain. They fly away, and who can follow them with the senses of the flesh? Who can grasp them, even when they're close by? The sense of the flesh is slow because it's a physical sense, and is limited by the flesh. It's sufficient for the end for which it was made, but it doesn't suffice to stop things running toward their appointed end. For in your word, by which they are created, they receive their commission, "This far you may come, and no farther" (Job 38:11).

Don't be foolish, my soul, and don't deaden the ear of your heart with the din of your folly. And listen! The Word himself calls you to return to that place of rest where love isn't abandoned if it doesn't first abandon itself. Some things pass away so that others may replace them, and so this lower universe is made complete in all its parts. "But do I ever depart?" asks the word of God. Fix your dwelling there; trust whatever you have there, my soul, for now you're worn out with deceits. Entrust to truth whatever you have from the truth, and you'll lose nothing. What is decayed in you will flourish again, and all your diseases will be healed. Your body, that part of you that perishes, will be re-formed and renewed, and restored to you again. It won't drag you down to where it is laid, but will abide with you before God, who continues and lives forever.

Why then, my soul, be perverse and follow your flesh? Let it turn and follow you instead. Whatever you feel through it is only a part of the whole. Feeling only the parts, you don't know the whole, yet you're delighted by them. If the senses of the flesh had the capacity for comprehending the whole, and if they hadn't been justly restricted to parts of the whole, you'd wish that all the parts would pass away, so that the whole might better please you. For what we speak, you hear by the same sense of the flesh, and you wouldn't want each syllable to remain. Rather you want them to fly away so that other syllables may follow and the whole be heard. So it is. When anything is made up of different parts, all of which don't exist together, they would please you more if they could all be perceived at once than if they are considered separately. But far better than these is the One who made the whole. He is our God. God doesn't pass away, and there is no one to take God's place.

If physical things please you, then praise God for them, but return your love to the One who created them, for fear that in the things that please you, you displease him. If souls please you, love them in God; for in themselves they are changeable, but in God they are firmly established. Without him they pass away and perish. In God, then, love them and carry along with you to him as many souls as you can, and say to them, "Let's love God, let's love God; he made the world and isn't far from it. He didn't make all things and then leave them, but they are from him and in him.

See, God is found wherever people love truth. He is within the very heart, yet the heart has strayed from him. Return to your heart, sinners, and hold fast to the One who made you. Stand with him and you'll stand fast. Rest in him and you'll be at rest. Where do you go in these rugged paths? Where do you go? The good that you love is from him. But it's good and sweet by being referred to him, and it will become bitter if you forsake him for it. Why, then, do you still wander in these difficult and trying ways? There's no rest where you're trying to find it. Try to find what you're searching for, but it isn't where you're searching for it. You're trying to find a blessed life in the land of death; it isn't here. How could there be a blessed life where there is no life?

Our true Life came down to this earth, and bore our death and killed it out of the abundance of his own life. Thundering loudly, he called to us to return to him into that secret place from which he came forth to us—coming first into the Virgin's womb, where humanity was joined to him, our mortal flesh, that it might not be forever mortal, and from there, "like a bridegroom coming out of his chamber, like a champion rejoicing to run his course" (Psalm 19:5). For he didn't delay, but ran, calling loudly by words, deeds, death, life, descent, ascension, crying loudly for us to return to him. And he departed from our sight, so that we might return to our heart and find him there. He departed, but, he's here! He wouldn't remain with us, yet he didn't leave us. He went back to the place he never left, because "the world was made through him" (John 1:10). He was in this world, and he "came into the world to save sinners" (1 Timothy 1:15). My soul confesses to him and he heals it, for it has sinned against him.

You children, how long will you be so slow of heart? Even now, after life has come down to you, will you not come up and live? But to where will you come up, since you're already in a high place, and have set your mouth against the heavens? First come down, that you may come up, and come up to God. For you've fallen by rising against him.

Tell your friends this, so that they may weep in this valley of tears. Draw them to God with you, because it's by God's Spirit that you speak to them this way, if as you speak you're glowing with the fire of love.

I didn't know these things then, and I loved those lower beauties. I was sinking into the very depths, and I said to my friends, "Do we love anything but what is beautiful? What then is the beautiful? And what is beauty? What is it that attracts and unites us to the things we love? For unless they contain a grace and beauty, they could by no means attract us to them." And I noticed and perceived that in the objects themselves there was one beauty by themselves alone, and another that depended on their mutual relationship with the whole, as a part of a body with its whole, or a shoe with its foot, and so on. This all came to my mind out of my inmost heart, and I wrote books (two or three, I think) entitled *On the Beautiful and the Fitting*. You know how many, God, but I've forgotten. I don't have them, for they've strayed from me, I forget how.

What was it that prompted me, Lord my God, to dedicate these books to Hierius, an orator of Rome? I didn't know him by sight, but I loved him for the fame of his learning and recognition, and for some of his words I had heard, which pleased me. He pleased me because he pleased others, who praised him highly, amazed that a Syrian, first taught in Greek eloquence, should become a wonderful Latin orator and one so learned in philosophy. Therefore he was commended and loved, though we've never seen him. Does this love come into the heart of the hearer from the mouth of the one who praises him? Not at all. But through one who loves, another's love is set ablaze. This is why we love the one who is commended when we believe that the praise comes from a sincere heart; that is, when the praise is from one who truly loves him.

At that time I loved people on the judgment of others, not upon yours, my God, in whom no one is deceived. Why didn't I love them for qualities like those of the renowned charioteer, or the great fighter with wild animals in the amphitheater, whose popularity and fame spread far and wide? Although I admired them, I didn't care to be like them. I had no desire to be praised and liked as actors are, even though I myself praised and loved them. I would have chosen to remain unknown rather than to be known as they were, and even hated rather than loved as they were.

How are these various and different loves distributed in one soul? Why, since we're all equal, do I love in another what I would hate to be? It doesn't follow, since a good horse is loved by one who wouldn't choose to be a horse even if he could, that the same may be said of an actor, since we're both sharing the same nature. Human beings are very deep, and you number our hairs, Lord. Not one of them falls without you. And yet the hairs of our heads are more easily numbered than are our feelings and the movements of our hearts.

But that orator whom I admired so much was the kind of man I wanted to be myself. I strayed through inflated pride, and I was "blown here and there by every wind" (Ephesians 4:14), yet you steered my course, though very secretly. I know very well now and I confess to you with sure confidence that I loved him more for the praise he received from others than for the things for which he was being praised. If he had been criticized, and those same people had disapproved of him, and had told the very same things about him with scorn and contempt, I would never have been inspired and drawn to love him. His qualities would have been no different, only the attitude of these who spoke about him.

See how the soul lies helpless and flat with the face down, reduced to extreme weakness and incapacitation when it isn't yet stayed on the firmness of truth! The winds of speech blow from the breasts of the opinionated, and we're carried this way and that, driven forward and backward. The light is obscured to us, and the truth isn't seen. Yet, there it is in front of us.

It was a great concern to me that my style and ideas should be known to that man. If he approved, I would be filled with more admiration for him. But if he disapproved, this egotistical heart of mine, void of your stability, would have been offended. And yet, I reflected with pleasure on my book entitled *On the Beautiful and the Fitting* that I wrote to him, and viewed it and admired it—though no one else joined me in doing so.

I didn't yet see how this great subject of the beautiful and the fitting turns upon your wisdom, Almighty One, for you alone do great wonders. My mind ranged through physical forms. I defined and distinguished as "pleasing" that which is so in itself; and I defined as "fitting" that which is beautiful in its relationship and fitness to some other thing, and I supported this by physical examples.

I turned my attention to the nature of the mind, but the false notions I had of spiritual things prevented me from seeing the truth. The very force of truth flashed into my eyes, but I turned away my thirsty soul from nonphysical substance to line, colors, and shapes. Because I couldn't see these in my mind, I concluded that I couldn't perceive my mind. And since I loved the peace in virtue and hated the discord in immoral acts, I distinguished a kind of unity in the first and a sort of disunity in the other. I visualized that the rational soul, the nature of truth and the highest good were all included in that unity.

 Augustine has been discussing the difference between eternal things and earthly, temporary things, and now he is shifting into a long (and difficult) section exploring evil. He makes the transition by asking the Big Questions: Did

*God create evil, or does God merely allow evil to happen?
If God creates or allows evil, does that mean that God
changes?*

In the disunity, unfortunately I imagined there was some unknown substance of irrational life. I thought the nature of the greatest evil was only a substance, but had real life, too, and that it didn't come forth from you, my God, from whom all things exist. The first I called a Monad, as if it were a soul without gender. The other I called a Duad— anger, deeds of violence, in deeds of passion and lust—not knowing what I was talking about. For I hadn't known, nor had I been taught, that evil isn't a substance. nor is our soul that chief and unchangeable good.

For just as in the case of violent deeds, if the emotion of the soul from which the impulse comes is depraved and thrusts itself arrogantly and shame- fully, and as it is in acts of passion when the emotion of the soul is unrestrained in its fleshly desires—so also, errors and false opinions contaminate our life if the rational soul itself is depraved, as mine was then. I didn't know that the soul must be enlightened by another light to be partaker of truth, since it isn't itself the essence of truth. "You, LORD, keep my lamp burning; my God turns my darkness into light" (Psalm 18:28). "Out of his fullness we have all received" (John 1:16). For you are "the true light that gives light to everyone" (John 1:9). You "do not change like shifting shadows" (James 1:17).

Though I pressed toward you, I was thrust back from you, so that I might taste of death, for you "oppose the proud" (1 Peter 5:5). And what was prouder than for me to maintain with a marvelous madness that I myself was by nature what you are? For since I was subject to change (that much was very clear to me, my very desire to become wise being the desire of the worse to change for the better), still I chose to imagine that you were subject to change rather than to see myself not to be what you are. Therefore I was repelled by you, and you resisted my pride. So I went on making mental images of physical forms.

Being flesh, I accused the flesh; and being "a passing breeze" (Psalm 78:39), I didn't return to you, but kept on wandering toward things that have no being, neither in you, nor in me, nor in the body. They weren't created for me by your truth, but they were made up out of physical things by my vanity.

I used to ask your faithful little ones, my fellow citizens (from whom I was in exile, though I didn't know it)—and I used to ask flippantly and foolishly, "Why does the soul fall into error if God created it?" But I wouldn't allow anyone to ask me, "Why then, does God fall into error?" I maintained that your unchangeable substance was forced to make an error rather than to confess that my changeable substance had gone astray through its own fault, and now lay in error for its punishment.

I was about twenty-six or twenty-seven years old when I wrote these books, meditating on the physical images that clamored in the ears of my heart. These I directed, sweet truth, to your inward melody, meditating on "the beautiful and the fitting," longing to stay and listen to you, to be glad to hear the bridegroom's voice (Matthew 25:6), but I couldn't. By the voices of my own errors I was driven forth, and by the weight of my own pride, I was sinking into the lowest pit. For you did not "let me hear joy and gladness" nor did "the bones . . . rejoice" that were not yet humbled (Psalm 51:8).

Aristotle lived from 384–322 BC, and he was one of the greatest philosophers ever. In his early book Categories, *he proposes that all things fall into one or more of these ten categories: substance, quantity, quality, relation, place, time, position, state, action, and passion.*

And what good did it do me, that when I was barely twenty years old, a book of Aristotle's entitled *The Ten Categories* fell into my hands? I hung on its very name as something great and divine, since my teacher who taught rhetoric at Carthage and others who were considered to be educated, referred to it with cheeks swelling with pride. I read it by myself and understood it without anyone's help. And on conferring with others, who said that they had hardly understood it with the aid of capable tutors who not only explained it verbally, but drew many things in the sand, they could tell me no more about it than I had learned by reading it alone.

The book appeared to me to speak very clearly of substances, such as human beings; and of features, such as the figure, shape and size, and height; and of a man's relationship, whose brother he is; or where placed, when born; whether he stands or sits; wears shoes or armor, or is doing something or having something done to him—and all the other countless things that might be classed under these nine categories—of which I have given some examples, or under that chief category of substance.

How did all this help me? Imagining that whatever existed was included in those ten categories, I tried to understand you, my God, your wonderful and unchangeable unity in the same way, as if you were subject to your own greatness or beauty; so that they should exist in you as their subject, as it is in bodies—whereas you yourself are your own greatness and beauty. But a material body isn't great or pleasant because it's a body, since it wouldn't stop being a body if it were smaller or less beautiful. But what I conceived of you was falsehood, not truth—fictions of my misery, not the realities of your blessedness. For you had commanded and it was done in me, that the earth should bring forth thorns and thistles for me, and that by the sweat of my brow I should eat my food (like Adam and Eve in Genesis 3:19).

What did it help me that all the books I could find of the so-called liberal arts, I could read and understand by myself, I who was a slave of evil affections? I took delight in them, not knowing the

One from whom came all that was true or certain in them. I had my back to the light and my face toward the things enlightened, so even when I discerned things enlightened, my face itself wasn't enlightened. Whatever was written either on rhetoric or logic, geometry, music, or arithmetic, I understood without any great difficulty and without any instructor, as you know, Lord my God, because both quickness of understanding and acuteness in discerning were your gifts. Yet I didn't give you thanks for them. So they didn't do me any good; they harmed me, since I desired to get so great a share of my substance into my own power. I didn't reserve my strength for you, but went away from you into a far country, to waste my substance on lusts (like the prodigal son in Luke 15:13).

What good was it to me to have good abilities if I didn't put them to good use? For I didn't perceive that those arts were attained with great difficulty even by the studious and talented, until I attempted to explain them to others; and the one who could follow my explanations most easily was considered the most proficient in them.

But what good did this do me while I supposed you, Lord God, who are the Truth, to be a vast and bright body, and I a fragment of that body? My perverseness was too great! But that's how I was. I'm not embarrassed, my God, to confess before you your mercies toward me, and to call on you, I who wasn't embarrassed then to profess my blasphemies before men and to bark against you. Of what good to me was my quick wit in those sciences and all those knotty volumes that I unraveled without human help, seeing that I was so disgustingly wrong and was so full of sacrilegious shamelessness in the doctrine of devotion and reverence? A far slower wit did more good for your little ones. They didn't depart from you. In the nest of your Church they could safely become fledged and nourish the wings of their charity by the food of a sound faith.

Lord our God, under the shadow of your wings let us hope. Protect us, and carry us. You'll carry us when we're little, and even down to our gray hairs you'll carry us; for when you are our strength, then it truly is strength; but when it's our own, then it's weakness. Our good lives only with you; when we're averted, we're perverted. Let us now, Lord, return, so that we may not be overturned; because with you good lives without any decay, for you are that good. We don't need to be afraid that because we fell away from that good, we'll find no place to which we can return; for when we left it, our home, your eternity, didn't fall.

Chapter Five

At Twenty-nine

 Whereas the last chapter took us through an entire decade of Augustine's life, he now slows down the pace considerably, and the next chapters will contain his reflections on a year each.

Accept the sacrifice of my confessions by the means of my tongue, which you've formed and have prompted to confess to your name. "Heal me, LORD, for my bones are in agony" (Psalm 6:2), and let them exclaim, "Who is like you, LORD?" (Psalm 35:10). One who confesses to you doesn't inform you what takes place within him, since a closed heart doesn't shut out your eye, neither can our hardheartedness repulse your hand. For you dissolve it at will, either in pity or in vengeance, and "nothing is deprived of your warmth" (Psalm 19:6).

Let my soul praise you, so that it may love you. Let it confess your mercies before you, so that it may praise you. Your whole creation never ceases to praise you—the spirit of every person whose voice is directed to you, all created things, animate and inanimate, by the voice of those who meditate on them, so that our souls may ascend to you from their weariness, and leaning on those things that you've created, pass beyond them to you, who made them wonderfully. Refreshment and true strength are there.

Let the restless and the wicked depart and run away from you. You see them and pierce through the darkness. Everything with them seems pleasant, but they're polluted. How have they injured you? In what have they disgraced your rule, which is just and perfect from heaven to the lowest earth? Where did they run away to when they ran away from your presence? Or where do you not find them? They ran away so that they might not see you seeing them, and in their blindness might stumble into you, because you forsake nothing that you've made, so that the wicked, I say, might stumble upon you, and be justly hurt. Withdrawing themselves from your gentleness, and stumbling at your uprightness, they fall upon their own roughness. In truth they don't know that you, whom no place shuts in, are everywhere, and that you alone are near even to those who remove themselves far from you.

Let them then be turned and search for you, because you haven't forsaken your creatures as they have forsaken their Creator. Let them be turned and search for you, and see, you're there in their hearts, in the hearts of those who confess before you and cast themselves upon you, and weep on your bosom, bearing in mind all their stubborn ways. Then you gently wipe away their tears, and they weep still more, and delight in their weeping, since you, Lord—not a human of flesh and blood, but you, Lord, who made them—now remake and comfort them. Where was I when I was searching for you? You were there before me, but I had gone away even from myself. I couldn't find myself, much less you!

Let me now lay before my God my twenty-ninth year. A certain bishop of the Manicheans named Faustus had come to Carthage, a great snare of the devil. He entangled many through the lure of his sweet language.

 Here Augustine begins a long section describing his growing discomfort with the beliefs of Manicheism, particularly with its faulty science.

Though I commended his speech, I couldn't separate myself from the truth I was so eager to learn. I wasn't so much concerned with the small dish of speech but with the knowledge that this Faustus, so praised among them, might set before me to feed on. His fame had already informed me that he was skilled in all valuable learning, and especially learned in the liberal sciences.

Since I had read and could remember much of the philosophers, I used to compare some of what they had written with those long fables of the Manicheans. What the philosophers taught seemed to me more probable, even though they could only pertain to this lower world. They could by no means find the Lord in it. "Though the LORD is exalted, he looks kindly on the lowly, but he takes notice of the proud from afar" (Psalm 138:6). You draw near to the repentant in heart, not to the proud—no, not even if by cunning skill they could count the number of the stars and the sand, and measure the starry regions and trace the courses of the planets.

With their understanding and the capacity that you've given them, the philosophers search out these things. They've found out much. They foretold, many years before, eclipses of the sun and moon, what day and hour and minute. Their calculations didn't fail, but it happened as they foretold. They wrote down the rules they had found out, and people read them to this day. From them others can foretell in what year, month, day and hour, and at what quarter of its light the moon or sun will be eclipsed; and so it will happen just as predicted.

Those who don't know this art are in awe and are astonished at this, and those who know it are glad and are exalted. By an ungodly pride, departing from you, forsaking your light, they foretell an eclipse of the sun's light long before it will happen, but they don't see the eclipse of their own light that's already present. For they don't search religiously where their intelligence comes from. And when they find out that you made these things, they don't give themselves to you so that you may preserve what you made, nor do they offer to you what they have made themselves. They don't put to death their own soaring pride, *as birds of the air*, nor their own curiosities, by which, like *the fish of the sea*, they wander over the unknown paths of the deep hole. Nor do they curb their own extravagances, like *beasts of the field*; so that you, Lord, you who are a consuming fire (Hebrews 12:29), might burn up those dead cares of theirs and renew them to immortality.

But they didn't know your Word, the way by which you created these things that they number, and those who number them, and the ability to perceive and the understanding by which they can number. They don't know that "your understanding has no limit" (Psalm 147:5). But the only Begotten himself "has become for us wisdom from God— that is, our righteousness, holiness and redemption" (1 Corinthians 1:30), and has been numbered with us (Isaiah 53:12), and paid tribute to Caesar (Luke 20:25). They didn't know this way by which they might descend to him, not that through him they might ascend to him. They didn't know this way and fancied themselves exalted among the stars and shining. You see, they fell to the earth, and "their foolish hearts were darkened" (Romans 1:21).

They say many true things concerning the creation; but Truth, the Architect of creation, they don't reverently try to find, and therefore they don't find him. Or if they find him, knowing him to be God, they don't glorify him as God, neither are thankful, but become egotistical in their imaginations and claim themselves to be wise, attributing to themselves what is yours. At the same time, with a perverse blindness, they attribute to you their own qualities, forging lies about you who are the truth, and they "exchange the glory of the immortal God for images made to look like mortal human beings and birds and animals and reptiles . . . and worship and serve created things rather than the Creator" (Romans 1:23–25).

I retained many truths from people concerning the creation, and I saw their theories confirmed by calculations, the succession of seasons, and the visible evidence of the stars. I compared them with the sayings of Manicheus, who in his frenzy had written many books on these subjects, but I didn't discover any account of the solstices, or equinoxes, or the eclipses of the greater lights, or anything of the kind I had learned in the books of secular philosophy. But I was ordered to believe Manicheus, even though what he wrote didn't correspond to what had been established by mathematics and by my own sight. His account was very different.

Lord God of truth, does the person who knows these things please you? Surely, one is unhappy who knows all these and doesn't know you. But how happy are those who know you even though they may not know these things. Those who know both you and them aren't happier on account of them, but only on account of you, if knowing you they glorify you as God, give thanks, and don't become egotistical in their thoughts. But they are happier who know how to own a tree and give thanks to you for the use of it—although they may not know how many feet high it is, or how wide it spreads—than the one who measures it and counts all its branches, but neither owns it nor knows or loves its creator.

Even so, a just person to whom all the world of wealth belongs, and who, as having nothing, yet possesses all things by holding fast to you whom all things serve, though he doesn't even know the circles of the Great Bear [that is, the Big Dipper constellation], is no doubt in a better state than one who can measure the heavens, number the stars, and weigh the elements, but is forgetful of you who "arranged all things by measure and number and weight" (Wisdom 11:20 RSV).

Who ordered this Manicheus to write on all these things, the knowledge of which wasn't necessary for devotion and reverence? For you've told us that "the fear of the Lord—that is wisdom" (Job 28:28). Manicheus might have been ignorant of this even if he had had perfect knowledge of created things; but since he had no knowledge of these things, yet most impudently dared to teach them, it's clear that he had no acquaintance with the fear of the Lord.

Even if we have knowledge of worldly matters, it's foolish to make a profession of them. Confession before you is our duty. It was for this reason that Manicheus spoke much of these things, but was convicted by those who had truly learned them, that what understanding he had in other, more difficult matters might be brought into question. He didn't want to be lightly esteemed, but went about trying to persuade others that the Holy Spirit, the Comforter and Enricher of your faithful people, was resident in him with full authority. So when it was discovered that his teaching about the heavens and stars and the movements of the sun and moon was false (although these things don't pertain to the teaching of religion), his sacrilegious presumption would become plain enough, since he spoke of things that not only did he not know, but that were false, and did so with such flagrant vanity of pride that he would try to attribute them to himself as to a divine person.

When I hear a Christian friend ignorant of these things, and mistaken on them, I can bear patiently with such a person holding to their opinions. I don't think any ignorance as to the position or character of this material creation can injure them as long as they don't believe anything unworthy of you, Lord, the Creator of all. But it does injure them if they imagine it to pertain to the essence of divine doctrine, or still hold too strongly to that of which they're ignorant. Yet even such a weakness in the infancy of faith is supported by charity, our mother, while the new self grows up into a mature person, so as not to be "blown here and there by every wind of teaching" (Ephesians 4:14).

But Manicheus presumed to be at once the teacher, author, head, and leader of all he could induce to believe him, so that all who followed him believed that they followed not a mere man, but your Holy Spirit. Who wouldn't judge that, when once he was convicted of having taught anything false, he should be despised and utterly rejected? But I hadn't yet clearly determined whether the changes of longer and shorter days and nights, and day and night itself, with the eclipses of the sun and moon, and whatever else of the kind I had read of in other books, could be harmonized with his words. If by any means they could, I would still have questioned whether his theories were true or not, although I might, on account of his reputed holiness, have continued to rest my faith upon his authority.

For almost all those nine years during which, with unsettled mind, I had been a Manichean disciple, I was looking forward very eagerly to the coming of this Faustus.

Many Manicheans who couldn't answer Augustine's increasingly difficult questions assured him that an expert named Faustus would be able to, but Augustine found Faustus' answers just as weak.

For the other members of the sect, whom I had chanced to meet, when they couldn't answer the questions I raised, always held out to me the coming of this Faustus, when these and greater questions would be most readily and abundantly cleared up in conference with him. Then when he came, I found him to be a man of pleasant speech, who could speak fluently and in better language, but yet he said the very same things the others had said.

To what avail was a more elegant cupbearer, since he didn't offer me the more precious drink for which I was thirsty? My ears were already filled with such things, and they didn't seem more convincing to me because they were expressed better; nor were they true because they were eloquent; nor was the soul wise because the face was handsome and the language eloquent. Those who praised him highly to me weren't competent judges. They thought he was prudent and wise because he was pleasing in his speech. I was aware, however, that another kind of person is suspicious even of truth itself, if it comes in smooth and flowing language.

But you, my God, had already instructed me in wonderful and secret ways. I believe that it was you who taught me, because it is truth, and there is no teacher of truth besides you, wherever or from whatever direction it may dawn on us! From you, therefore, I had now learned that a thing shouldn't be considered true because it's well spoken, nor untrue because it comes from a stammering tongue. Neither should it be considered true because it's delivered unskillfully, nor untrue because the language is fine. Just as wholesome and unwholesome food may be served either in elegant or plain dishes, so wisdom or foolishness may come in either elegant or simple language. Either kind of food may be served up in either kind of dish.

The eagerness, then, with which I had waited so long for this man was delighted with his manner and attitude when we conversed, and with the fluent and appropriate words he used to express his ideas. I was delighted then, and along with many others (and even more than others) I praised and acclaimed him.

It annoyed me, however, that in the meetings of his hearers I wasn't allowed to introduce, into a familiar exchange of discussion with him, the questions that troubled me. When I was able to speak, and began with my friends to engage him in conversation, and had mentioned the questions that perplexed me, I found him first utterly ignorant of the liberal sciences except grammar, and even that only in an ordinary way. But because he had read some of Cicero, a very few books of Seneca, some writings by the poets and the few volumes of his own sect that were written in Latin, and was practiced speaking every day, he had acquired a certain eloquence that proved more pleasing and enticing under the control of a ready wit and a kind of natural grace.

Was it not as I recall it, Lord my God, Judge of my conscience? My heart and my memory are laid open before you. You directed me by the hidden mystery of your providence, bringing those shameful errors of mine before my eyes, so that I might see them and detest them.

After it became clear to me that Manicheus was ignorant of the arts in which I had thought he excelled, I began to despair of Faustus' clearing up and explaining the difficulties that bothered me. Although he was ignorant of these, he might still have held the truths of godliness if he hadn't been a Manichean. Their books are filled with lengthy fables about the sky, the stars, the sun and moon, and I had ceased to believe that he was able to show me in any satisfactory way what I so earnestly desired—whether, on comparing these things with the mathematical calculations I had read elsewhere, the accounts given in the books of Manicheus were preferable, or at least as good.

When I suggested this to be considered and discussed, he was modest enough to shrink from the burden of it. He knew that he didn't know these things and wasn't ashamed to acknowledge it. He wasn't one of those talkative persons, many of whom I had been troubled with, who attempted to teach me these things and said nothing. This man had a heart, and though it wasn't right toward you, it wasn't false toward himself. He wasn't altogether ignorant of his own ignorance, and he wouldn't rashly entangle himself in a controversy from which he could neither retreat nor extricate himself gracefully. For that reason I liked him better. The modesty of a frank and honest mind is more beautiful than the acquaintance of the knowledge I desired—and that's how I found him to be in all the more difficult and subtle questions.

My eagerness for the writings of Manicheus having been blunted, I despaired even more of their other teachers. Since Faustus, who was so well known among them, had turned out as he had in the various things that troubled me, I began to occupy myself with him in the study of literature in which he was greatly interested, and which I as a professor of rhetoric was teaching young students at Carthage. With him I read either the books he expressed a wish to hear, or those I thought suited his bent of mind. But all my efforts by which I had planned to advance in that sect came utterly to an end by my acquaintance with that man. It wasn't that I separated myself from them altogether, but, finding nothing better, I decided to content myself with what I had happened on in any way, unless by chance something more desirable should present itself.

 As he is leaving Manicheism, Augustine has not yet found anything to replace it, so he admits to following a mishmash of religious beliefs, taken from several religions (which, in fact, is what Manicheism is).

Therefore Faustus, the snare of death to so many, had, without willing or knowing it, now begun to loosen the trap in which I had been caught. Your hands, my God, in the secret purpose of your providence, didn't forsake my soul. Out of my mother's heart's blood a sacrifice was offered to you for me, her tears pouring forth day and night. You dealt with me in marvelous ways. It was you who did it, my God: "The LORD makes firm the steps of those who delight in him" (Psalm 37:23). For how will we obtain salvation if not from your hand, remaking what it has made?

It was by your dealing with me that I was persuaded to go to Rome to teach there what I had been teaching at Carthage. And how I was persuaded to do this, I won't fail to confess before you, for the profoundest workings of your wisdom and your ever-present mercy to me must be pondered and acknowledged.

I didn't wish to go to Rome because greater advantages and higher dignities were guaranteed me by the friends who persuaded me to it (though these things did have an influence over my mind at that time). My chief and almost only reason was that I heard that young people studied there more quietly and they didn't disrespectfully rush into the class of a teacher who wasn't their own whenever they liked. They weren't even allowed to enter without his permission.

At Carthage, on the other hand, there reigns a most disgraceful and unruly lack of restraint among the students. They burst in rudely, and with the wildest gestures they interrupt the order that anyone has established for the good of his scholars.

They commit all kinds of outrages with an amazing insensitivity that would be punishable by law if custom didn't support them. That custom shows them to be all the more worthless, because they think that what they do is now lawful, though it will never be lawful by your unchangeable law, and they think they are doing it with impunity. Their very blindness is their punishment, though, and they suffer far worse things than they do themselves. The manners, then, that I wouldn't adopt as a student, I was compelled as a teacher to endure in others; and so I was only too glad to go to a place where all who know anything about it assured me these things weren't done.

But you, "my refuge, my portion in the land of the living" (Psalm 141:6) prodded me while I was at Carthage, that I might be torn from it, while you offered me enticements at Rome by which to attract me there, by people who loved this dying life, the one doing insane things, the other promising vain and useless things. To correct my path, you secretly employed their perversity and mine. For those who disturbed my tranquility were blinded by a shameful madness, and those who drew me elsewhere smelled and tasted of the earth. And I, who hated my real misery in one place, was trying to find a false happiness in another.

You knew, Lord, why I left one country to go to the other, yet you didn't show it either to me or to my mother, who grievously wept for my going and followed me as far as the sea. But I deceived her when she tried desperately to hold me back by force, determined either to keep me back or go with me. I pretended that I had a friend whom I couldn't leave until he had a favorable wind to set sail. I lied to my good mother and got away. But you've mercifully pardoned me for this, saving me, so filled with abominable defilements from the waters of the sea, for the water of your grace. By your grace, when I was cleansed [in the waters of baptism], the fountains of my mother's eyes would be dried, the tears with which she daily watered the ground under her face. When she refused to return without me, it was with difficulty that I persuaded her to spend that night in a place not far from our ship, where there was a chapel in memory of the blessed Cyprian. That night I secretly left while she remained praying and weeping.

What was it, Lord, that she asked of you with so many tears, but that you would not allow me to sail? But you, in the depths of your counsels, and hearing the real purpose of her request, didn't grant what she was asking then, in order to make me into what she more deeply desired.

 Augustine, his girlfriend, and their child secretly leave for Rome, and that presumably leaves Monica's prayers for his salvation unfulfilled.

The wind blew and filled our sails, and the shore disappeared from our sight. The next day she was there, wild with grief, filling your ears with complaints and groans, which you disregarded. All the while, by means of my longings, you were speeding me to the end of all longing; and the earthly part of her love for me was being disciplined by the just punishment of sorrow. She loved to have me with her, as mothers do, but even more than many do, and she didn't know what great joy you were preparing for her by my absence. Not knowing this, she wept and mourned, and in her agony showed the inheritance of Eve—searching in sorrow for what she had brought forth in sorrow. And yet, after laying blame on my treachery and cruelty, she took up her intercessions for me with you again, and returned home, while I went on to Rome.

When I got to Rome, I was welcomed with the severe punishment of bodily illness, and I very nearly fell into hell, burdened with all the sins that I had committed against you, myself, and others—many and grievous sins—over and above that load of original sin by which we all die in Adam (1 Corinthians 15:22).

 Here Augustine recounts his second near-death experience from another fever.

For you had not forgiven me any of these things in Christ, neither had he abolished by his Cross the enmity that I had incurred with you by my sins. For how could he by the crucifixion of a ghost, which was all I supposed him to be? The death of my soul then was as real as the death of his flesh seemed unreal to me. And if the death of his flesh was true, the life of my soul was false, since I didn't believe it. My fever increased, and I was at the point of dying and leaving this world forever. If I had gone then, where would I have gone but into the fiery torments my misdeeds deserved in the truth of your law?

My mother didn't know this, yet she prayed for me, far away. And you, who are present everywhere, heard her where she was, and you had pity on me where I was, so that I would regain the health of my body, though I was still sick in my grossly irreverent heart. In all that danger I didn't ask for your baptism, and I was better as a boy when I asked for it because of my mother's devotion and reverence, as I have already related and confessed. But I had grown up to my own dishonor, and I madly desired all the purposes of your medicine, which would not have allowed me, even such as I was, to have died a double death—the death of both body and soul.

 Of course, Monica's prayers were eventually answered, because Augustine did convert to Christianity. In possibly a bit of exaggeration here, Augustine compares her sufferings to that of the Virgin Mary, whose "soul was pierced" by the death of Jesus (see Luke 2:35).

If my mother's heart had been pierced with this wound, it could never have been healed. I can't sufficiently express the love she had for me, nor how she labored for me in the spirit with a far keener anguish than when she gave me birth in the flesh.

I can't conceive how she could have been healed if my death in sin had come to pierce the deepest heart of her love. Where then would have been those earnest, frequent and unceasing prayers of hers? You would not, God of mercies, despise the contrite and humble heart (Psalm 51:17) of that morally pure and prudent widow, so full of deeds of charity, so full of duty and service to your saints. Never for a day did she miss the offering of sacrifice at your altar both morning and evening, coming to your church, not for idle gossip and old wives tales, but so that she might hear you in your sermons and that you might hear her prayers. Could you—you by whose gift she was this way—despise and withhold your help from the tears of such a person, by which she begged you not for gold or silver, nor any changeable or fleeting good, but for the salvation of her son's soul? Never, Lord!

Yes, you were at hand, and you were hearing and acting in the way that you had determined previously that it should be done. Far be it from you that you should deceive her in your visions and the answers she had from you—some of which I have spoken of, some I haven't mentioned—that she had laid up in her faithful heart. Always praying, she pressed these on you as your own signature. For, because "your love endures forever" (Psalm 118:1), you condescend to those whose debts you've pardoned, to become a debtor yourself by your promises.

You restored me then from that sickness, and healed the son of your servant in his body, that he might live for you, to give to him a better and more enduring health. Even then at Rome I joined those deluding and deluded "saints" [the Manicheans]—not their "hearers" only (it was in the house of one of them that I had fallen sick and had recovered), but also with those whom they call "Elect." For I still thought that we're not actually the ones who sin, but that some other nature sins within us. And it gratified my pride to be free from blame. When I had committed any evil, I didn't confess that I had done it, so that you might heal my soul because it had sinned against you (Psalm 41:4), but I loved to excuse it, and to accuse something else (I don't know *what* other thing) that was within me but wasn't actually me. But in truth it was all me, and my ungodliness had divided against myself; and that sin was all the more incurable because I didn't judge myself to be a sinner.

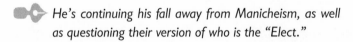 *He's continuing his fall away from Manicheism, as well as questioning their version of who is the "Elect."*

It was a despicable gross immorality, almighty God, that I would rather have you suffer defeat in me to my destruction rather than allow myself to be overcome by you to my salvation. You hadn't as yet set a guard over my mouth, and a watch over the door of my lips, so that my heart wouldn't be drawn to wicked speeches, to make excuses for sins with people who take part in wicked deeds (Psalm 141:3-4). Therefore I was still united with their "Elect."

Hopeless of becoming proficient in that false doctrine, I held more loosely and carelessly even those things with which I had resolved to rest contented if I could find nothing better. I was now half inclined to believe that the philosophers known as Academics were wiser than the others, in that they held that we ought to doubt everything, and taught that we can't comprehend any truth. This is what I thought they taught, as they are commonly held to do, not yet realizing their meaning. I didn't hesitate freely and openly to discourage my host from that over-confidence I perceived in him toward the fictions that fill the Manichean books. Yet I lived in closer friendship with them than with others who weren't of this heresy. But I didn't defend it with my former eagerness.

Still, my intimacy with that sect, many of whose followers lived secretly in Rome, made me hesitant to try to find any other way—especially in your Church, Lord of heaven and earth, Creator of all things visible and invisible. They turned me away from it, and it still seemed very uncivilized to believe that you had the form of human flesh and were confined by the bodily features of our members. When I wanted to think about my God, I didn't know what to think of but a mass of bodies, for I thought that anything other than such a mass was nothing. This was the greatest and almost only cause of my inevitable error.

I also believed that evil was a similar sort of substance, and that it had its own foul and misshapen bulk—whether it was dense (which they called earth), or thin and tenuous, like the air (which they imagine to be some evil mind creeping through the earth). And because my devotion and reverence, such as it was, constrained me to believe that the good God never created any evil nature, I conceived two masses, opposed to one another, both infinite, but the evil one more contracted, the good one more expansive. The other offensive beliefs followed from this destructive beginning. For when my mind tried to revert to the Christian faith, I was repulsed, because the Christian faith isn't what I thought it was.

 Here he's continuing to question whether God actually created evil.

It seemed more devout to believe that you, my God (to whom I make confession of your mercies) were infinite on all sides except that side where the mass of evil was opposed to you (there I was compelled to consider you to be finite), than if I should imagine you to be limited on all sides by the form of a human body. It seemed better to me to believe that you had created no evil—which in my ignorance I thought was not only a substance, but a bodily one. This was because I had no conception of the mind except as an extremely thin body, diffused through space. And this seemed better than to believe that the nature of evil, such as I considered it to be, could have come forth from you.

Our very Savior himself, your only begotten Son, I believed to have been brought forth for our salvation out of the mass of your most shining substance. So I didn't believe anything about him except what I was able to imagine in my vanity. I thought, then, that such a nature couldn't have been born of the Virgin Mary without being mixed with her flesh. And I couldn't see how the nature that I had pictured to myself, could be mixed with humanity without being contaminated. Therefore I was afraid to believe that he was born as a human for fear that I would have to believe that he was contaminated by the flesh. Now, your spiritual people will smile kindly and lovingly at me if they read these confessions of mine. Yet this is how I was.

I thought the things the Manicheans had criticized in your Scriptures couldn't be defended. Sometimes I wanted to discuss these different points with someone very well learned in those books to find what he thought of them. The speech of a man named Elpidius, who had spoken and disputed face to face with the Manicheans, had begun to affect me, even when I was at Carthage. From the Scriptures he produced many arguments that weren't easy to dispute, and the Manicheans' answers to them seemed weak to me. They preferred not to give their answers publicly, but only to us in private, maintaining that the Scriptures of the New Testament had been tampered with by some unknown hand who wanted to firmly plant the Jewish law on the Christian faith. But they themselves didn't produce any uncorrupted copies. Still thinking in terms of physical bodies, however, I was held captive, oppressed, and to a degree suffocated by the concept of those masses, gasping for the breath of your truth, which I wasn't able to breathe pure and untainted.

Then I began to conscientiously practice what I had come to Rome to do—teach rhetoric. First, in my house I gathered some people to whom and through whom I had begun to be known. And then I learned that in Rome other offenses were committed to which I hadn't been exposed in Africa. True, as I had been told, those riotous disruptions by reckless young men weren't practiced here. But I was told that all of a sudden, in order to avoid paying their teacher his fees, a number of them would conspire together and go off to another teacher—breakers of faith, who for the love of money hold justice cheap. My heart hated them, but not with a perfect hatred. Perhaps I hated them more because I was to suffer by them, than because they did things that were completely against the law. In truth, these low-lifes are unfaithful to you by loving the fleeting mockeries of temporal things and shameful gain that fouls the hand that grasps it, clinging to this passing world and despising you. You stay put and call back and forgive the two-timing human soul when it returns to you.

I still hate perverse and crooked persons of this type, though I love them if they can be corrected to the point where they prefer the learning they acquire to the money, and prefer learning of you, God; you who are the truth and the fullness of assured good, the purest peace. But I disliked them then for my own sake rather than wanting them to become good for your sake.

When a message came from Milan to Rome to the prefect of the city requesting a teacher of rhetoric for that city to be sent at public expense, I applied for the job. I did this through the same persons, still intoxicated as I was with worthless Manichean concepts, in order to be freed from those very concepts, though neither they nor I knew it at the time. They recommended that Symmachus, the prefect, test me through a speech on some subject and then send me on to Milan.

Milan is a city in northern Italy, and at that time the famous Ambrose was the bishop there. Ambrose was a great churchman, and he's considered one of the church fathers.

I went to Milan then, to Ambrose the bishop, known to the whole world as one of the best men, a devout servant of yours. His eloquent conversation in those times dispensed plentifully the flour of your wheat, the gladness of your oil, and the sober exhilaration of your wine to your people. I was unknowingly led to him by you, that knowingly I might be led to you by him. That man of God received me like a father, and as a bishop gave a kindly welcome at my arrival. I began to love him, not at first as a teacher of the truth (something I utterly despaired of finding in your Church), but as a man who was friendly to me.

I listened earnestly to him as he preached to the people, not with the motive I should have had, but, so to speak, testing his eloquence, to see if it truly measured up to its fame or was greater or less than others had claimed for it. I hung intently on his *words*, but I was a careless and scornful spectator of their *meaning*. I was delighted with the charm of his speech, though it was less cheerful and soothing in manner than that of Faustus. As to the content, there could be no comparison, however; Faustus was wandering in the midst of Manichean delusions, while Ambrose was teaching salvation. But "salvation is far from the wicked" (Psalm 119:155), such as I was then. Yet little by little I was drawing nearer without knowing it.

I took no pains to learn what Ambrose preached, but only to hear how he spoke (for that pointless attention was all that I had left, despairing as I was of finding a way open to you). Yet, along with the words that I prized, there also came into my mind the ideas that I ignored, for I couldn't separate them. While I opened my heart to let in how eloquently he spoke, there also entered in how truly he spoke. But this was only by degrees.

 Remember that Augustine was writing this before there were anything but Catholic Christians—there were no

Protestants or Eastern Orthodox or anything else—
everyone was simply a Christian. The meaning of
"catholic" is "universal."

For the first time these things began to appear to me to be defensible, and the catholic faith, for which I had thought nothing could be said against the attacks of the Manicheans, I now began to see might be defended without embarrassment. This was especially so after I had heard Ambrose explain one or two places in the Old Testament, often allegorically, whereas when I had understood them literally, they had killed me spiritually. When many of these passages had been explained this way, I started to disapprove of my despair at believing that no reply could be made to those who hated and scoffed at the Law and the Prophets. Yet I still didn't see that the catholic way could be supported by learned advocates who could defend it adequately and answer objections with some show of reason. I also didn't know that what I held to be true should therefore be condemned, because both sides seemed to me to be equally defensible. The catholic cause didn't appear to me to be defeated, but neither did it seem to have won yet.

I proceeded to devote my thoughts to see if I could in any way convict the Manicheans of falsehood through any certain proof. If I could have conceived of a spiritual substance, all their strong points would have crumbled and been cast utterly out of my mind. But I couldn't. As I considered and compared things more and more, concerning the physical body and the whole of nature that the senses of the body can grasp, I judged that the opinions of the philosophers were much more probable.

So in what I thought was the manner of the Academics—doubting everything and wavering among all—I settled on this much: that I must leave the Manicheans. After much consideration, I determined that while I was in such doubt I couldn't remain in that sect, since I already preferred some of the philosophers to it. I completely refused to commit the cure of my sick soul to the philosophers, however, because they were without the saving name of Christ. I determined then, to become a catechumen

 A catechumen was a term often used in the ancient Church to describe what churches today often call a person in confirmation class: Not yet confirmed, but in a process of learning. The word comes originally from Galatians 6:6.

in the catholic Church, to which I had been commended by my parents, till something certain should manifest itself to me by which I might better steer my course.

Chapter Six

More Secular Concerns and Ambitions

Hope of my youth, where were you at this time in my life; where had you gone? Hadn't you created me and made me different from the beasts of the field and the birds of the air? You made me wiser than they are, yet I walked in dark and slippery places. I searched for you outside myself and didn't find the God of my heart. I had come into the depths of the sea, and distrusted and despaired of ever discovering the truth.

By this time my mother had come to me, strengthened by her devotion and reverence, following me over sea and land, and trusting you through all danger. In the perils of the sea, she even comforted the sailors, who were more used to comforting the passengers who were unfamiliar with the sea when they were frightened. She assured them that they would arrive safely, because you had given her this assurance in a vision.

She found me in deadly trouble through my despair of ever finding the truth. But when I told her that I was no longer a Manichean, though not yet a catholic Christian, she wasn't overjoyed, as if she were hearing a happy surprise. For she had already been reassured concerning that part of my distress for which she had grieved over me as if I were a dead person, but also as a person who would be raised to you. She had carried me in her thoughts as if I were on a funeral bier on my way to the grave. And this was so that you might say to the widow's son, "Young man, I say to you, get up!" (Luke 7:14), and he would revive and begin to speak, and you would deliver him to his mother.

Her heart wasn't shaken with some sort of turbulent euphoria when she heard that what she had endeavored to obtain from the Lord daily with so many tears was in so great a part already accomplished.

 Here you might say that Augustine has "one foot in the boat" of the Christian church, but it takes him another couple of years to get the other foot in....

For though I hadn't come to the truth yet, I'd been rescued from falsehood. Since she was confident that you, who had promised the entire thing, would one day give the rest, she replied to me most calmly and with a heart full of faith that she believed in Christ and that before she departed this life she would see me a catholic believer.

She said this much to me. But to you, who are the fountain of mercies, she poured forth more abundant prayers and tears, that you would speed up your help and fill my darkness with light. She hurried all the more eagerly to the church, hanging on the words of Ambrose, praying for the "spring of water welling up to eternal life" (John 4:14). She loved that man as an angel of God (Galatians 4:14), because she knew that through him I had been brought to the inquiring state of faith I was now in. And she anticipated most confidently that I would pass through it from sickness to health after the onslaught, so to speak, of a sharper "high fever" like the one that physicians term the "crisis" (that leads to the breaking of the fever)

One time when my mother brought some cakes, bread, and wine to the chapels built in memory of the saints, as was her custom in Africa, the doorkeeper stopped her. As soon as she learned that the bishop had forbidden her, she reverently and obediently complied with his wishes. I myself wondered at how readily she blamed her own custom rather than question his prohibition. For drinking had not taken hold of her spirit, nor did the love of wine provoke her to hatred of the truth, as it does with too many men and women who revolt at a lesson of sobriety as much as drunken persons would revolt at a drink of water.

It was a custom in the Roman pagan religion to hold an annual banquet at the gravesite of a loved one, and to pour wine into the ground over the grave as an offering. Augustine's mom, Monica, had performed a similar ritual to this in her church, but then she was forbidden from continuing it by her bishop.

But when she had brought her basket with the customary festival food, in order to take a small taste of it herself and then give the rest away, she never allowed herself more than one small cup of wine, diluted according to her own temperate palate, and she would do that only out of courtesy. And if there were many chapels of departed saints to be honored in that way, she would carry around that same cup and use it everywhere. Not only did this make it very watery, but also it became unpleasantly warm by being carried about. She would distribute this cup to those about her in small sips, for she was looking for devotion, not pleasure.

So as soon as she found out that this custom had been forbidden even to those who would use it with moderation, by that famous preacher and most reverent and devout high-ranking clergyman, for fear that it would become an occasion of excess to people who become drunk, and because these festivals in honor of the dead so greatly resembled the superstition of pagans, she willingly abstained from it. In place of a basket filled with fruits of the earth, she learned to bring to these martyrs' chapels a heart filled with more purified prayers. Therefore she gave all she could to the poor, so that in this way, the communion of the Lord's body might be celebrated in the places where, following the example of his suffering, the martyrs had been sacrificed and rewarded with crowns.

Yet it seems to me, Lord my God, as you know my heart, that perhaps she wouldn't have yielded so readily to giving up this custom if it had been forbidden by someone else whom she didn't love as much as she loved Ambrose. And that's because she loved him most dearly for the sake of my salvation.

And he loved her, too, for her highly religious way of life, for she often did good works at the church in "keeping her spiritual fervor" (Romans 12:11). When Ambrose saw me, he would often burst forth into praise of her, congratulating me that I had such a mother, little knowing what kind of son she had in me. But I doubted all these things and thought that the way of life couldn't be found.

I didn't yet groan in prayer, so that you would help me, but my spirit was wholly intent on knowledge and eager to argue. I considered Ambrose to be a happy man, as the world counts happiness, because he was held in honor by such great people. Only his celibacy—his not being married and abstaining from sex—seemed to me a painful burden. I couldn't guess, nor had I experienced what hope he carried within him, what struggles he had against the temptations that attacked his honor, or what comfort in adversity and what sweet joys your bread gave him as he fed on it in the hidden depths of his heart.

Nor did he know the heat of my desires or the depth of my danger. I couldn't ask him what I needed to as I would have liked, because I was kept from talking with him by crowds of busy people to whose weaknesses he devoted himself. The small periods of time when he wasn't engaged with those people, he used to refresh either his body with necessary sustenance or his mind with reading. But when he was reading, his eye glided over the pages and his mind searched out the meaning, but his voice and tongue were silent. Often when we had come (for no one was forbidden to enter, and it wasn't his practice to have anyone announced to him), we saw him reading this way to himself, and never any other way. Having long sat in silence (for who would dare interrupt one so intent?) we were inclined to leave, concluding that in the few moments he had free from the demands of others' business, he was unwilling to be distracted from the renewal of his mind.

Perhaps he was afraid that if the author he was reading expressed himself vaguely, some attentive and perplexed hearer might want him to explain it, or to discuss some of the harder questions. So he couldn't get through as many volumes as he desired if he spent his time in any other way. Also, the need to preserve his voice, which was very easily made hoarse, may have been the real reason for his reading to himself. But whatever his reason for doing so, certainly in such a man, it was a good one.

In any case, I had no opportunity to inquire from that holy spokesman of yours what was in his heart, unless the question could be answered briefly. The strong passions in me would require his full time and attention for me to pour them out to him, and I never found that time. Indeed, I heard him every Lord's day, "correctly handling the word of truth" (2 Timothy 2:15) among the people, and I was more and more convinced that all those knots of crafty slander that our [Manichean and Platonist] deceivers had tied against the holy books could be unraveled.

 Augustine is still hung up on the Christian idea that God could take on a bodily form in the person of Jesus of Nazareth. This idea is highly contrary to the philosophical views of Plato that he was following at the time.

And when I finally understood that the words "human beings created in the image of God" weren't understood by your spiritual children (whom you've mothered anew by the Church through grace) to mean that they believed you to be limited by a human shape—although what the nature of a spiritual substance could be I didn't have the faintest or weakest notion—I blushed with joy that for so many years I had growled, not against the catholic faith, but against the fictions of worldly imaginations. I had been so reckless and wicked in this that I had condemned ignorantly what I ought to have learned. For you, most high and most near, most hidden yet most present, don't have limbs, some larger, some smaller, but you are wholly everywhere, yet nowhere in space. You're not of such bodily shape, yet you made us after your own image; and yet, we're confined in space from head to foot.

Not understanding how you could have an "image" in which human beings could be created, I should have knocked (Matthew 7:7) and expressed my doubt as to how to believe it instead of insultingly opposing it as if it were as I understood it. The sharper the doubts that gnawed at my heart, the more ashamed I became to think that I had been deluded and deceived so long by the promise of certainties, and that with childish error and rashness I had talked long and foolishly about so many uncertainties as if they were true. It hadn't yet become clear to me that they were completely false. However, I was certain that they were uncertain, and that I had formerly held them to be certain, when with a blind contentiousness, I had accused your Church.

Though I hadn't yet discovered that your Church teaches the truth, I knew at least that it didn't teach what I had so vehemently accused it of teaching. So I was confounded and converted. I was glad, my God, that the one Church, the body of your only Son, where the name of Christ had been put on me as an infant, had no taste for these childish trifles. Furthermore I found that it didn't in its sound teaching maintain that you, the Creator of all, occupy the immensity of space, yet are bounded on all sides by human form.

I was glad, too, that the Old Testament scriptures of the Law and the Prophets were set before me. I was no longer approaching them from the viewpoint from which they had previously seemed absurd, when I condemned your saints for thinking what they didn't actually think. With delight I often heard Ambrose say in his sermons to the people, as though he were earnestly commending it as a rule of interpretation, "The letter kills, but the Spirit gives life" (2 Corinthians 3:6). He would then draw aside the mystical veil, laying open spiritually what according to the letter seemed to teach something unsound.

Augustine attended Ambrose's church almost every Sunday while he lived in Milan, and the bishop's sermons help Augustine understand many of the parts of the Christian gospel that confused him.

His teaching contained nothing that offended me, though I didn't know yet whether or not it was true. I kept my heart from agreeing to anything, fearing to fall headlong into something I wasn't comfortable with yet. But by hanging in suspense, I was in worse shape. I wanted to be as certain of things I couldn't see as I was that seven plus three equal ten. I wasn't so crazy as to think that even this could be known for sure. But I wanted to have other things as clear as this, whether they were physical things that my senses couldn't grasp, or spiritual ones that I didn't know how to conceive of, except physically.

By believing, I might have been cured, so that once the eyesight of my soul had been made clear, I might have been led to your truth, which lives forever and fails in nothing. But just as a person who has tried a bad physician is afraid to trust a good one, so it was with my soul, which could only be healed by believing. For fear that it should believe falsehoods again, it refused to be cured. So I resisted your hands, the hands of the One who prepared the medicines of faith for us and applied them to the diseases of the whole world, and gave them such great power.

From this time, I preferred catholic doctrine. I felt that the Church acted more modestly and honestly, when it required people to believe things that can't be proved—whether they can be proved only to some people, or can't be proved at all— whereas, among the Manicheans, our disposition to believe too readily was mocked by a promise of sure knowledge. So many of the most fantastic and absurd things were forced on us to believe them because they couldn't be proved.

After that, Lord, little by little, with a most gentle and merciful hand, drawing and calming my heart, you persuaded me to consider the innumerable things I believed that I had neither seen nor was present to see when they happened. These include many things in secular history, the numerous reports of places and cities that I hadn't seen, so many things told me by friends, by doctors, and by others. If we didn't believe what others tell us, we would do nothing at all in this life. Finally, I thought of how firmly I believed that I was born of two particular parents, something I couldn't know unless I believed what I heard.

Taking all this into consideration, you persuaded me that it wasn't those who believe your books, which you've established with such great authority among nearly all nations, but those who didn't believe them who were to be faulted. I wasn't to listen to those people who say to me, "How do you know that those books have been given to humankind by the Spirit of the one true and most true God?" For this very thing was above all to be believed, since no argument of all that multitude of blasphemous questionings that I had read in the self-contradicting philosophers could wring from me the belief that you exist—though what you are I didn't know—and that the government of human affairs belongs to you.

This much I believed, sometimes more strongly than other people. Yet I always believed both that you exist and that you have a care for us, though I was ignorant of how to think of your substance and of what way led back to you. So since we're too weak to discover truth by our unaided reason, and since we need the authority of Holy Scripture, I had now begun to believe that you would never have given such excellence of authority to Scripture in all lands if you hadn't willed that people should search for you and believe in you through them.

For those things in the Scripture whose strange meanings used to offend me, now that many of them were satisfactorily explained, I ascribed to the depth of the mysteries. And the authority of the Bible seemed to me all the more esteemed and worthy of religious belief in that while it was open to all to read, it reserved the majesty of its mysteries within its deeper meaning. Stooping to all in great plainness of its language and simplicity of style, it yet calls for the most intense application of serious minds. In this way it might receive all with open arms. And though narrow passages carry a few people toward you (Matthew 7:13-14)—yet there are many more of that type of person than if it didn't stand on such high authority, or draw multitudes into its arms by its holy humility. I continued to think about these things, and you were with me. I sighed, and you heard me. I vacillated and you guided me. I roamed through the broad way of the world, but you didn't forsake me.

I longed for honors, money, and marriage, and you laughed at me. In these desires I underwent the bitterest of crosses, but in this you were too gracious to me to allow anything to grow sweet to me that wasn't yourself. See my heart, Lord, for it's your will that I remember all this and confess it before you. Let my soul hold tight to you, now that you've freed it from the tenacious hold of death. How miserable it was! You touched the center of the wound, so that forsaking all else, my soul might be converted to you, who are above all, and without whom all things would be nothing, so that it might be converted and healed.

How miserable I was, and how you dealt with me, to make me feel my misery on that day when I was preparing to recite a speech eulogizing the emperor! In it I was to utter many a lie, and to be applauded by those who knew I was lying. My heart was very troubled with a sense of guilt and boiling with the fever of consuming thoughts.

For, while walking along one of the streets of Milan, I observed a poor beggar. I suppose he had just eaten—he was joking and happy. I sighed and spoke to the friends around me about the sorrows that our ambitions bring us. For by such efforts as those in which I was then laboring, dragging along the burden of my own unhappiness, and making it worse by dragging it with me, I only searched for the happiness that beggar had, but possibly might never again attain it. What he had gotten by means of a few coins begged from others, the joy of a temporary happiness—I was scheming for by many a torturous twisting and turning.

To be sure, the beggar's happiness wasn't true happiness. Yet with all my ambitions I was searching for a happiness that was even more untrue. For he was happy, while I was anxious. He was carefree, I was full of fears. But if anyone had asked me, would I rather be cheerful or fearful, I would answer, cheerful. Again, if I were asked if I would rather be as the beggar was, I would have chosen myself, even with all my cares and fears—out of perversity. But would this be wise and reasonable? I ought not to prefer myself to him because I was more educated than he was, since all my education didn't make me happy, but I only attempted to please others by it. In this way you "crushed my bones" (Psalm 51:8) with the rod of your correction.

Get away from my soul, then, all those who say to it, "It makes a difference where a man's happiness comes from. That beggar was glad in his drunkenness; you longed to be glad in glory." What glory, Lord? Glory that isn't in you is no true glory; and it overthrew my soul more than his false happiness. For he would digest his drunkenness that night, but I had slept and risen again with mine, and was to sleep again and again, to rise with it, how many days!

It makes a difference where a person's joy comes from. I know it, and the joy of a faithful hope lies far beyond such emptiness. Yes, he had surpassed me then. Truly he was happier, not only because he was thoroughly drenched in fun, while I was torn to pieces with cares, but also because by giving good wishes he had obtained wine, and I was trying to gain empty praise by lying. I said much of this to my good friends, and I often noticed in them what I was feeling then, that when it went badly

with me, I grieved and doubled the problem. And
if any prosperity smiled on me, I was reluctant to
seize it, for almost before I could grasp it, it flew
away.

*Here Augustine begins a long section in which he praises
his close friends Alypius (pronounced a-LIP-ee-us) and
Nebridius (ne-BRI-dee-us). Nebridius had died by the
time Augustine wrote this, and Alypius had converted
and been baptized on the same day as Augustine.*

We who were living as friends together com-
plained about things, but I talked about this mainly
and most intimately with Alypius and Nebridius.
Alypius came from the same town as I did , his
parents being of the highest rank there. He was
younger than I, and had studied under me, first
when I taught in our home town, and later at
Carthage. He thought a great deal of me, because I
seemed kind and educated to him, and I loved him
for his instinctive love of virtue, which was remarkable in someone so young.

Yet the whirlpool of Carthaginian customs had
drawn Alypius into the madness of the gladiatorial
games. In Carthage these frivolous spectacles are
followed passionately. When he first became
embroiled in that pitiful addiction, I had a public
school and was teaching rhetoric there. Because of
some ill feeling between his father and me, he wasn't
attending my classes. Seeing how fatally he was
doting on the circus games, I was deeply grieved

that he seemed about to throw away his great promise, if, indeed he hadn't already done so. Yet I had no means of advising or reclaiming him with any sort of constraint, either by the kindness of a friend or with the authority of a teacher. For I assumed he thought of me the same way his father did. But he didn't. He put aside his father's will in the matter and began to greet me, sometimes coming into my classroom to listen a little and then leaving.

I had put out of my mind any thought that I could deal with him to prevent the undoing of so good a mind through a blind and headstrong passion for vain and useless pastimes. But surely you, Lord, who guide the course of all you have created, hadn't forgotten this man who was to be one day one of your children, and a bishop in your Church.

And so that Alypius' conversion might plainly be attributed to you, you brought it about through me without my knowing it. For as I sat one day in my usual place with my students in front of me, he came in, greeted me, sat down, and turned his attention to what I was saying. By chance I was dealing with a certain passage, when a comparison borrowed from the circus games occurred to me, as being appropriate to make what I wanted to convey plainer and more pleasant, seasoned with a biting jibe at those who had become slaves to that madness.

You know, God, that I wasn't thinking then of curing Alypius of that plague. But he took it to himself and thought that I said it simply for his sake. What another would have taken as an occasion of offense with me, that right-minded young man took as a reason to be offended at himself and to love me more warmly. You said long ago, and it's written in your Book, "Rebuke the wise and they will love you" (Proverbs 9:8). I hadn't rebuked him, but you make use of all people, with or without their knowledge, to the purpose that you know. You made burning coals out of my heart and tongue (Ezekiel 1:13), to set on fire and heal that young man's hopeful mind that was wasting away. "We will not hide . . . the praiseworthy deeds of the LORD" (Psalm 78:4), which from my inmost soul I confess before you. For after that speech, Alypius rushed out of that deep pit into which he had been willfully plunged, blinded with its miserable pastimes. He roused his mind with resolute self-control. As a result, all the filth of the circus games fell away from him, and he never returned to them again.

After this he prevailed upon his reluctant father to let him become my pupil. He gave way, and consented. Alypius, beginning to hear me again, became involved in the same superstition that he believed was true and genuine. But it was a senseless and seducing ploy, ensnaring precious souls who weren't able yet to reach the height of virtue, and were easily beguiled with the veneer of what was only a shadowy and counterfeit virtue.

Pursuing the worldly course that his parents had urged him to follow, Alypius had gone to Rome before me to study law. There he was carried away with an incredible passion for the gladiatorial shows. While at first he utterly detested these spectacles, one day by chance he met several of his acquaintances and fellow-students coming from dinner. With a friendly violence, they forced him along with them into the amphitheater. He resisted and vehemently protested, "Though you may drag my body into that place and set me down, can you force me to turn my mind or my eyes to those shows? I will be absent though present, and will overcome both you and them." Hearing this, they led him on, nevertheless, possibly wanting to test him, to see whether he could do as he said.

When they got there and had taken such seats as they could find, the whole place became excited with the inhuman sport. He closed his eyes and forbade his mind to show interest in such evil. If he had only shut his ears also! For in the fight, when one fell, a mighty cry of the whole crowd stirred him strongly. Overcome by curiosity, as if ready to despise and rise above whatever it might be, even when he looked at it, he opened his eyes, and was struck with a deeper wound in his soul than the gladiator that he had wanted to see had received in his body.

In this way he fell more miserably than the one whose fall had occasioned the great noise. That noise, entering through his ears and unlocking his eyes, struck and beat down his soul, which was bold rather than resolute, and weaker because it presumed on itself when it ought to have relied on you. For as soon as he saw that blood, he drank down a sort of savageness with it. Nor did he turn away, but fixed his eyes, drinking in madness unawares, delighted with the guilty fight and drunk with that bloody pastime.

He was now no longer the man who had come in, but was one of the crowd he had come to—and a true companion of those who had brought him. Why say more? He looked, shouted, was excited, and carried away with him the madness that would stimulate him not only to return with those who first drew him there, but even without them, yes, and to draw in others. But from all this you pulled him abruptly away with a most strong and most merciful hand, and taught him to place his confidence not in himself, but in you. But that was later.

This experience was being stored up in his memory to be a medicine later on. So, too, was the following incident that happened when he was studying under me at Carthage. At noon he was meditating in the marketplace on what he had to recite (as scholars used to do). You allowed him to be apprehended by the officer of the marketplace as a thief. I think you allowed it for no other reason than that he, who would later prove to be so great a man, should begin to learn that in judging cases, one shouldn't swiftly condemn another with a reckless disposition to believe too readily.

As he was walking up and down by himself before the judgment seat, with his notebook and pen, a young man, one of the scholars—the real thief—secretly carrying a hatchet, unseen by Alypius, got in as far as the lead gratings that protect the silversmiths' shops. He began to cut away the lead, but the noise of the hatchet alerted the silversmiths below, and they sent men to take whomever they should find into custody. But the thief, hearing their voices, ran away, leaving his hatchet, afraid to be caught with it.

Now Alypius, who had not seen the man enter, noticed him leaving, and saw how fast he made off. Wanting to know more of what was going on, he entered the place, and finding the hatchet, he stood wondering and considering it, when suddenly, those who had been sent caught him alone, hatchet in hand. They seized him, dragged him away, and gathering the tenants in the marketplace together, boasted of having captured a notorious thief. He was led away to appear before the judge.

But this was the end of his lesson. For immediately, Lord, you came to the aid of his innocence, of which you were the only witness. As he was being led away to prison or punishment, they were met by a certain architect who had charge of the public buildings. They were especially glad to see him, for he used to suspect them of stealing the goods that disappeared out of the marketplace, as though they could at last show him who the real thief was. This man had seen Alypius often at a certain senator's house, where he often called to pay his respects. Recognizing him at once, he took him aside by the hand and asked the occasion of such a great calamity, heard the whole matter, and commanded the rabble present (who were causing a great tumult with their shouts and threats) to go with him.

It happened that they passed the house of the young man who had committed the theft, and in front of the door was a boy young enough to be likely to reveal the whole story, not sensing any harm to his master. Alypius remembered that this boy was with the thief in the market-place, and told the architect. Showing the hatchet to the boy, he asked him whose it was. "Ours," he said immediately; and being questioned further, he told the whole story. In that way the crime was transferred to that house, and the crowd, which had been hurling insults at Alypius, was shamed. And the one who would someday be a preacher of your Word and a judge of numerous cases in your Church, went away better experienced and instructed.

I found Alypius at Rome and we became close friends. He went with me to Milan, so that he might still be with me to practice something of the law he had studied more to please his parents than himself. He had already sat as assessor three terms with an honesty that made others marvel. On the other hand, he marveled at others who could prefer gold to honesty. His character was tested, not only with the bait of greed, but with the goad of fear. At Rome he was assessor to the count of the Italian treasury. There was at that time a very powerful senator to whose favors many stood indebted, and who was feared by many. He wanted a thing granted him that was forbidden by the laws, such as his power usually achieved. Alypius resisted him. With all his heart he refused his proffered bribes. Threats were made, but he trampled them under his feet.

All the while, people were astonished at so rare a spirit that neither desired the friendship nor feared the enmity of one so powerful and so widely known for the innumerable means he had of doing good or evil. And the very judge for whom Alypius worked as advisor, although also unwilling that the thing should be done, didn't dare openly refuse this senator, but put the matter off on Alypius, claiming that he wouldn't allow him to do as the senator wished. And in truth, if the judge had tried to do it, Alypius would have resigned from his court.

There was one thing in the way of learning by which he was very nearly seduced, that he might have books copied for him at government expense. Thinking about the justice of this, however, he changed his mind for the better, considering the integrity that hindered him to be more valuable than the power that permitted him to do it. These are little things, but "whoever can be trusted with very little can also be trusted with much" (Luke 16:10). Nor can the truth possibly be in vain that came out of your mouth, "If you have not been trustworthy in handling worldly wealth, who will trust you with true riches? And if you have not been trustworthy with someone else's property, who will give you property of your own?" (Luke 16:11-12)? This is the man he was, the one who was so close a friend and wavered in purpose, as I did, about what course in life he should take.

 Here Augustine shifts from writing about Alypius to Nebridius.

Nebridius had also left his native country near Carthage, and Carthage itself, where he used to live. He left behind his fine family estate, his house, and his mother who wouldn't follow him. He had come to Milan for no other reason than to live with me in a passionate search for truth and wisdom. Like me he sighed, and wavered, a fervent seeker after true life and a very acute examiner of the most difficult questions. There we were—three needy youths sighing out their poverty of spirit to one another, waiting upon you that you might "give them their food allowance at the proper time" (Luke 12:42). And in all the bitterness that by your mercy followed our worldly affairs, and in all the darkness that met us when we attempted to know the reason for those things, we said, "How long will this go on?" We often said this, but saying it, we didn't forsake these affairs, for as yet we had discovered nothing certain that we might embrace when we abandoned what we knew.

I wondered for a long time, anxiously reviewing what had happened since my nineteenth year, when I had first begun to burn with a desire for wisdom, resolving to abandon all empty hopes and vain and useless desires when I had found it. Now I was in my thirtieth year, stuck in the same filthy muck, greedy to enjoy fleeting pleasure, saying to myself, "Tomorrow I'm going to find wisdom; and it will appear plainly, and I'm going to understand it. See, Faustus will come and explain everything! You great men, you Academicians, is it true then, that nothing certain can be attained to guide one's life?

"But let me search more diligently and not despair. Look! Things in the church books that once seemed absurd don't appear so now, but may be honestly understood in other ways. I'm going to take my stand where my parents placed me as a child until the clear truth is discovered.

"But where should I look for it, and when? Ambrose has no free time. I have no free time to read. Where will I find the books? When and from where can I obtain them? From whom could I borrow them?

 This begins a long section of inner dialogue for Augustine —notice the quote marks. Think of an angel sitting on one shoulder and a devil on the other.

Let times be set, certain hours for the health of my soul. A great hope has dawned on us that the catholic faith doesn't teach what I thought and vainly accused it of teaching. The Church's learned ones hold it an abomination to believe that God is limited by the form of a human body. Do I doubt that I should knock, in order that the rest may be opened (Matthew 7:7)? My mornings are taken up with my students; what do I do with the rest of the day? Why don't we set our minds to this? But when, then, could we visit our great friends, whose favors we need? When could I prepare the lessons the students pay for? When could we refresh ourselves and relax our minds from the pressure of work?

"Perish everything! Dismiss these empty, vain things! I'm going to focus only on the search for truth! Life is miserable, death is uncertain. If it steals me away suddenly, what state am I going to be in when I go away, and where am I going to learn what I've neglected here? Will I suffer punishment for this negligence? What if death should cut off and completely put an end, along with thought itself, to all feeling and care? This too must be examined. But God forbid that it should be so! It isn't an empty thing. It isn't without reason that the lofty authority of the Christian faith has spread throughout the whole world. Never would so great a thing have been brought about by God for us if with the death of the body, the life of the soul came to an end. Why, then, am I delaying to abandon worldly hopes and give myself wholly to searching for God and the blessed life?

"But wait! Worldly things are pleasing. They have sweetness. I mustn't give them up lightly, for it would be embarrassing to return to them again.

Look how easy it is now to obtain some position of honor, and what more could I want? I have a group of influential friends. If nothing else comes along, at least a governorship may be offered me, and a wife with some money so she wouldn't be an added expense. And so I would have reached the height of my desires. Many great men who are most worthy of imitation have applied themselves to the study of wisdom in the state of marriage."

While I talked over these things, and these winds shifted and drove my heart this way and that, time passed on. But I delayed in turning to the Lord. From day to day, I postponed living in you, but I didn't postpone dying in myself every day. Loving a happy life, I was afraid to search for it in its own place, but searched for it by running away from it. I thought I would be too miserable if I couldn't be enfolded in a woman's arms. And I didn't think of your mercy as a healing medicine for that infirmity, not having tried it. As for continence—that is, abstinence from sex, I supposed it to be in our own power (though in myself I didn't find that power), being so foolish as not to know what is written, that no one can be continent unless you grant it (Wisdom 8:21 D-R). Certainly you would have given it if with heartfelt groaning I had shouted in your ears, and with a firm faith had cast my care upon you.

It was actually Alypius who kept me from marrying. He asserted that if I did, there was no way that we could live together with enough free time to search for the wisdom we had long desired. Even then he himself was so morally pure in his thoughts and conduct that it was wonderful—all the more so, too, since in his early youth he had gone astray, but he had felt remorse and revulsion at it, and from then on had lived in complete continence.

I opposed him with the examples of married men who had cherished wisdom and found favor with God, retaining their friends and loving them faithfully. But I fell far short of their greatness of spirit and was enslaved with the disease of the flesh. Its deadly sweetness dragged my chain along, dreading to be loosened, and as if it pressed my wound, rejected his good persuasions as if it were the hand of one who would unchain me. Moreover, the serpent spoke to Alypius himself through me, weaving and laying pleasurable snares in his path, in which his virtuous and free feet might become entangled.

He marveled that I, whom he esteemed so greatly, should be stuck so fast in the grip of that pleasure as to affirm whenever we discussed it that I could never lead an unmarried life. I urged in my defense, when I saw his surprise, that there was a great difference between his momentary and furtive experience of that life (which he hardly remembered and could so easily despise) and my continued acquaintance with it. It needed only the honorable name of marriage to be added, and then he wouldn't be astonished at my inability to abandon that way of life.

Then he began also to want to be married, not because he was overcome with lust for such pleasure, but out of curiosity. For he wanted to know, he said, what this thing was without which my life—which seemed so pleasant to him—should seem to be no life at all but a punishment. His mind, which was free from that chain, was astounded at my slavery, and through that amazement went on to a desire to try it.

 It is no secret that Augustine reacted strongly to his own youthful, sexual mistakes. He developed an idea that sexual pleasure is the same thing as lust, and he taught that even married couples should have sex only in order to procreate. So, when he says "slavery," here, he means that sort of lust.

From the desire, he was going on to the trial itself, and from there, he might have sunk into that slavery that at present he marveled at. He was willing to make a "covenant with death" (Isaiah 28:18), and "one who loves danger will perish in it" (see Ecclesiasticus 3:27 D-R). Whatever honor there is in the state of a well-ordered married life and the bringing up of children had only slight interest to us. As for me, it was for the most part trying to satisfy an insatiable lust; but Alypius was about to be led captive by curiosity. That's how we remained until you, most High, not forsaking our lowliness, had mercy on our misery and came to our aid by wonderful and secret ways.

Active efforts were made to get me a wife. I courted. I was engaged, largely through my mother's efforts, because once I was married, I was to be baptized, and she was glad that I was becoming more disposed to it every day. She observed that her desires and your promises were being fulfilled in my faith. Then by my own request and her own desires, she asked you every day that you would show her something concerning my future marriage by a vision, but you wouldn't do it. She saw, indeed, certain meaningless fantasies, of the kind that the human spirit, preoccupied with such things, can conjure up. She told these to me, but not with the usual confidence she displayed when you showed her anything. For she could, she declared, discern between your revelations and the dreams of her own soul, through a certain feeling that she couldn't put into words. Yet the matter was pressed, and I asked a young woman to marry me. She was two years under the marriageable age. But since she was pleasing, I waited for her.

Many of us friends, conferring about and detesting the turbulent vexations of human life, had almost decided to search for a life of peace, apart from the bustle of humanity. This was to be obtained by bringing together whatever we might own separately and make one household of it all; so that through the sincerity of our friendship nothing would belong especially to any one of us, and everything would belong to everyone. We thought there might be ten people in this group, some of whom were very rich, especially Romanianus, from our town, who had been a close friend of mine from childhood.

Grave business matters had brought him up to court, and he was the most eager of us all for this project. His voice carried great weight in commanding it, because his ample estate far exceeded any of the rest. We resolved also that two officers should be chosen each year to provide everything necessary, while the rest were to be left undisturbed. But when we began to consider whether the wives, which some of us already had, and others hoped to have, would permit this, that entire plan, which was being so well formed, came to pieces in our hands and was utterly wrecked and cast aside. Then we fell again into sighs and groans, following the broad roads and beaten paths of the world (Matthew 7:13). Many thoughts were in our hearts, "but it is the LORD's purpose that prevails" (Proverbs 19:21). Out of your counsel, you laughed at ours, and prepared your own, purposing "give us our food at the proper time" and to "open your hand and satisfy the desire of every living thing" (Psalm 144:14-15).

Meanwhile my sins were being multiplied. My mistress was torn from my side because she was a hindrance to my marriage. My heart, which clung to her, was torn, wounded, and bleeding. She returned to Africa, vowing to you never to have sex with another man, leaving me with my illegitimate son by her. But unhappy as I was, I couldn't imitate her resolve. Impatient with delaying, since it would be two years before I could obtain the one I wanted to marry, not being so much a lover of marriage as a slave to lust, I took another mistress—not a wife, of course. In this way, by its enslavement to a lasting habit, my soul's disease was nourished and kept vigorous, or even increased until I should reach the sphere of marriage. The wound of my heart caused by the separation from my former mistress wasn't yet healed. After becoming inflamed and causing the most acute pain, it festered, and the pain became numbed, while I felt all the more hopeless.

To you be praise, to you be glory. Fountain of mercies! As I became more miserable, you were drawing nearer. Your right hand was continually ready to pull me out of the filthy muck and to cleanse me, but I didn't know it. Nothing called me back from a yet deeper gulf of sexual pleasures but the fear of death and of your judgment to come, which amid all my changes of opinion never left my heart. In a dispute with my friends, Alypius and Nebridius, on the nature of good and evil, I held that Epicurus would have, to my mind, won the argument if I hadn't believed that there remained a life for the soul after death and a place of making amends according to what we deserve, something that Epicurus didn't believe.

Epicurus (341–270 BC) was an ancient Greek philosopher who advocated indulgence in food, drink, and friends as a moral good. He didn't believe in the gods or in an afterlife.

"Supposing us to be immortal and to be living in the enjoyment of perpetual bodily pleasure without fear of losing it, why shouldn't we be happy, or what else should we be searching for?" I asked, not knowing that this very thing was at the heart of my misery. Being sunk and blinded as I was, I couldn't discern that light of excellence and beauty that we should embrace for its own sake. The human eye can't see it, but the inner person sees it. I also didn't consider how it was that I talked with pleasure on such foul subjects with my friends, while at the same time, I couldn't be happy without these friends, even in the midst of the greatest abundance of pleasures of the flesh. Yet I loved these friends for their sakes and I felt that they loved me for my own sake.

What crooked paths! How miserable is the audacious soul that hopes that by forsaking you it could gain some better thing! Tossed up and down, upon its back, its sides, and its belly, it finds only discomfort, for you alone are rest. And observe, you're near, to deliver us from our miserable wanderings and place us on your path. You comfort us and say, "Run. I will carry you; I will sustain you and I will rescue you" (see Isaiah 46:4).

Chapter Seven

Finding Plato on My Way
to Christianity

My evil and abominable youth was now dead,
and I was passing into early adulthood. As I
increased in years, I grew more defiled in emptiness, for I couldn't conceive of any substance but
such as I saw with my own eyes. I didn't think of
you, God, under the form of a human body. From
the time I began to hear anything of philosophy, I
had always avoided this, and I was glad to have
found the same rejection in the faith of our spiritual
mother, your Church. But I didn't know how else
to think of you.

As a human, and such as I was, I attempted to
conceive of you as the sovereign, only true God. In
my inmost soul I believed you to be incorruptible,
inviolable, and unchangeable. Though I didn't know

where or how, I saw plainly and felt sure that what can be corrupted must be inferior to the incorruptible.

 As Augustine recounts his foray into Neo-Platonism, you'll see the great dualities that are prevalent in that philosophy: The spirit is good and the body is bad, etc.

What couldn't be violated I preferred unhesitatingly to what could receive injury, and I deemed the unchangeable to be better than what is changeable. My heart passionately cried out against all my mental concepts, and with one blow I attempted to drive away from my mind's eye all the unclean ideas that buzzed around it.

But in the twinkling of an eye, these ideas gathered again thickly about me, flew against my face, and clouded my vision. So, even though I didn't think of you as having the form of a human body, I was forced to conceive of you as being something physical in space, either infused into the world or diffused infinitely outside it—a Being that was incorruptible, inviolable, and unchangeable. I preferred this to one that was corruptible, and violable, and changeable. For whatever I conceived to be deprived of this space seemed to me to be nothing—yes, altogether nothing, not even a vacuum. If a body were taken out of its place and the place should remain empty of any body at all, of earth and water, air and the heavens, it would still remain an empty space, a spacious nothing.

Being thus totally materialistically minded, I had no clear vision, even to myself. So that whatever wasn't extended over certain spaces, either diffused or massed together or puffed out, or whatever didn't or couldn't receive some of these dimensions, I thought was altogether nothing. My heart then ranged over such forms as I could see with my eyes. I didn't yet understand that this very observation by which I formed those same images was invisible to the eye, and yet my mind couldn't have formed them if it hadn't been some great thing itself.

In the same way I tried to conceive of you, who are the Life of my life, as vast, extending through infinite spaces, penetrating on every side the whole mass of the universe, and extending beyond it in every direction through immeasurable, boundless space. Thus the earth would hold you, the heavens would hold you, all things could hold you, and they would have their limits within you. Just as the sky above the earth doesn't hinder the light of the sun from passing through it, penetrating it, not by bursting or cutting, but by filling it wholly, so I imagined the body of the heavens, air, and sea, and earth, too, as being pervious to you, so that all its parts, the greatest and the smallest, admit your presence, and by a invisible inspiration you govern everything you've created, both inwardly and outwardly. This is what I conjectured, because I was unable to think of anything else. But this was false.

If this were true, then a greater part of the earth would contain a greater part of you, and a smaller one, less of you. And all things would be full of you in such a way that the body of an elephant would contain more of you than that of a sparrow, since it's larger and takes up more room. Therefore you would make parts of you present to the several parts of the world in fragments: large pieces to the large, small pieces to the small.

You're not like this, but you had not yet enlightened my darkness.

It was sufficient for me, Lord, to oppose those deceived deceivers, those speechless babblers (speechless, since your word didn't sound forth from them), to use the argument Nebridius used to propound while we were still at Carthage. All of us who heard it were disturbed by it at the time. It went like this: "What could that supposed kingdom of darkness, which the Manicheans consider a mass opposed to you, have done to God if he refused to fight with it?" If they answered that it would have done God some hurt, then God would be subject to injury and corruption. But if they said that it couldn't hurt God, then there was no reason why God should fight against it.

But, they held, it was this very fighting that involved some part of you. Some members or offspring of your very substance were intermingled with opposing powers and natures not created by you, and were corrupted and deteriorated to such an extent by them as to be turned from happiness to misery and to need assistance in order to be delivered and purified. This offspring of your substance, they taught, is the soul, which, enslaved, defiled, and corrupted as it is, can by your word be relieved, free, pure, and whole.

But Nebridius argued, "In that case, the word itself is corruptible, because it is of one and the same substance as the soul." And if they affirmed that our essential being (that is, your substance) is incorruptible, then all these sayings of theirs were false and deplorable. If they said that you're corruptible, then that very statement showed itself to be false and to be repulsed. This argument of Nebridius was an adequate one, then, against those who deserved to be vomited forth from a full stomach, since it gave them no escape from this dilemma without horrible blasphemy of heart and tongue, thinking and speaking such things about you.

But although I was fully persuaded that you were incorruptible and unchangeable, and in no part subject to alteration, Lord, the true God, who made not only our souls, but our bodies, and not only our souls and bodies, but all beings and all things, I still didn't understand, clearly and without difficulty, the cause of evil.

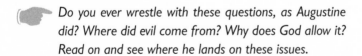 *Do you ever wrestle with these questions, as Augustine did? Where did evil come from? Why does God allow it? Read on and see where he lands on these issues.*

Whatever it was, I perceived that it must be understood not to force me to believe the unchanging God to be changeable, for fear that I would become the very evil I was searching to understand. I tried to understand it then, free from anxiety, sure of the untruthfulness of what was asserted by the Manicheans, whom I rejected with my whole heart. I saw that by trying to find the origin of evil they were filled with evil themselves in that they preferred to think that your substance allowed evil rather than that their own substance committed it.

So I directed my attention to discern what I had now heard—that free will is the cause of our doing evil, and your righteous judgment the cause of our suffering it. But I couldn't clearly discern it. When I tried to draw the eye of my mind out of that deep pit, I was plunged into it again. And as often as I tried, I was thrown back again. But this raised me a little toward your light, in that I now knew that I had a will as well as that I had life. When I was willing or was unwilling to do something, I was very certain that it was nothing and no one but myself who was willing or unwilling. Immediately I perceived that the cause of my sin lay there.

When I acted against my will, I saw that I suffered, and that I judged it not to be my fault, but my punishment. However, since I believed you to be most just, I quickly confessed that I was being justly punished.

Again I asked, "Who made me? Didn't my God who is not only good, but Goodness itself? How did I come then to will to do evil and to be unwilling to do good, so that I'm justly punished in this way? Who put this in me and implanted in me this "bitter root" (Hebrews 12:15), since I was completely created by my most sweet God? If the devil were the author of it, where did the devil himself come from? And if he was a good angel who became a devil by his own perverse will, where, again, did that evil will in him come from, seeing the whole nature of angels was made altogether good by that most good Creator?"

By these thoughts I was again sunk down and stifled. Yet I wasn't plunged into that hell of error (where no person confesses to you) to think that you personally participate in evil, rather than that people do it.

I was struggling to discover answers to other difficulties, having already found out that the incorruptible must be better than the corruptible. Whatever you were, I acknowledged you to be incorruptible.

 Still following Plato, Augustine considered anything that was material and therefore "corruptible" as necessarily a lower and worse form than anything that was spiritual and therefore "incorruptible."

No one ever was or ever will be able to conceive of anything better than you, who are the highest and best Good. But since the incorruptible is most surely and certainly to be preferred to the corruptible (as I now preferred it), then if you weren't incorruptible, it would have been possible for me to conceive of something better than my God.

As for corruptible things, I saw that I should search for you among them, and learn from them the origin of evil, that is, where the corruption comes from by which your substance can't be defiled. For by no necessity, by no unforeseen chance can this happen, because he is God, and what he wills is good, and he himself is that Good. But to be corrupted isn't good, nor are you compelled to do anything against your will, since your will isn't greater than your power. But it would be greater if you yourself were greater than yourself. For the will and power of God is God himself. And what can you not foresee, you who know all things? Nor is there any sort of nature that you don't know. Why should we give any more reasons for which the substance that's God can't be corruptible, since if it were so, it couldn't be God?

I kept searching for the origin of evil, but I searched for it the wrong way, and I didn't see what was wrong in my very search. I now set before the eye of my mind the whole creation, whatever we can see in it—the sea, earth, air, stars, trees, living creatures; and whatever we can't see, such as the vault of the heavens, all the angels, and all the spiritual inhabitants of heaven. My imagination placed all these, as if they were bodies, each in its own place. I made one huge mass of your creatures, differentiated according to the kinds of bodies—

some of them real bodies, some of them what I imagined spirits to be. I made this mass huge—not as it was, which I couldn't know, but as large as I thought sufficient, yet finite in every way. But I imagined you, Lord, surrounding it on every side through unmeasured space, nothing but an infinite sea; and it contained within it some sponge, huge, but finite, so that every part of the sponge would be filled with that immeasurable sea.

This is the way I conceived your creation to be, finite itself, filled with you, the Infinite. And I said, "Observe God, and see what he has created! And God is good, yes, most mightily and incomparably better than all these; but yet he, the Good, created them good. See how he encircles and fills them. Then where is evil, and where does it come from, and how did it creep in? What is its root and what is its seed? If it has no being at all, why then do we fear and avoid what has no being? If we fear it needlessly, then surely that very fear is evil, by which the heart is pricked and tormented—yes, and so much greater and evil, if we have nothing to fear, and yet do fear! Therefore, either the evil we fear exists, or our fear is evil.

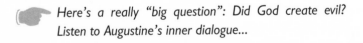 *Here's a really "big question": Did God create evil? Listen to Augustine's inner dialogue...*

"But then, where does it come from, seeing that God, the Good, has created all these things good? The greatest and chief Good has created all these lesser goods, but both Creator and created are all good. Where, then, is evil? Was there some evil matter out of which he made and formed and ordered it, yet left something in it that he didn't convert into good? If so, why? Did he lack the power to turn and change the whole lump, so that no evil should remain in it, seeing that he is all-powerful?

"Finally, why would God make anything at all of evil, and not instead by that same all-powerfulness cause it not to exist at all? Could it exist contrary to his will? If it existed from eternity, why did God allow it to be so through the infinite reaches of time in the past, and why was he pleased after so long a time to make something out of it? If he suddenly wanted to act, the Almighty should rather have acted so that this evil matter wouldn't exist at all, and so that he alone should be the whole, true, highest, and infinite Good. If it was good that the One who was good should also be the Framer and Creator of what was good, then having taken away and annihilated that evil matter, he might form good matter out of which to create all things. For God would not be all-powerful if he couldn't create something good without the aid of the matter that he himself hadn't created."

These thoughts turned over and over in my miserable heart, and I was overwhelmed and gnawed at by the fear that I would die before I had found the truth. Yet the faith of your Christ, our Lord and Savior, as it was held in the Church, was firmly fixed in my heart, although it was yet unformed in many points and diverging from the rule of right doctrine. My mind didn't utterly leave it, but drank in more and more of it every day.

By this time I had rejected the false fortunetelling and blasphemous absurdities of the astrologers. Let your own mercies, out of my very inmost soul, confess this also before you, my God. For who else calls us back from the death of all errors except the Life that can't die and the wisdom that, needing no light, enlightens the mind that needs it, and by which the universe is directed, even down to the fluttering leaves of the trees? You alone made provision to cure the obstinacy with which I struggled with Vindicianus, a keen old man, and Nebridius, a young man of remarkable talents. Vindicianus vigorously declared and Nebridius, though with some doubtfulness, often maintained that no art existed to foresee future things, but that human guesses were like a sort of lottery, and that out of many things that they predicted, some actually did happen without our predictors knowing that they would. They merely stumbled on these things by their numerous guesses.

You provided me with a friend, then, who frequently consulted astrologers, but who wasn't deeply versed in their lore. He was one who consulted them out of curiosity, and yet he knew something that he had heard from his father.

Here Augustine rejects astrology, even more common in his time than it is in ours.

He didn't know, however, how far his story would go in overthrowing my opinion of that art.

This man, Firminius by name, was a man of liberal education and well educated in rhetoric. He asked me, his friend, to interpret, according to his so-called constellations, some affairs of his in which his worldly hopes had risen. Although I had begun to lean toward Nebridius' opinion, I didn't altogether refuse to speculate about the matter and to tell him what came into my mind, undecided though it was. But I added that I was almost persuaded that these were only empty and ridiculous follies.

He then told me that his father had been very interested in astrological books, and had a friend as interested in them as himself. With joint study and consultation, they had fanned the flame of their affections for these foolish things so much so that they would observe the moments when dumb animals outside their houses gave birth to their young, and then observe the relative position of the heavens, to gather fresh proofs of this so-called art. He also said that his father had told him that when his mother was about to give birth to him [Firminius], a female slave of that friend of his father's was also pregnant at the same time. This couldn't remain unnoticed by her master, who took care with the most exact diligence to know the births even of his puppies. And so they did their calculations (one for his wife and the other for his servant), with the most careful observation, calculating the days, hours, and minutes.

It happened that both babies were delivered at the same moment, so that each had precisely the same horoscope, down to the minutest points, heir and slave alike. For as soon as the women began to be in labor, each man notified the other what was happening in their respective homes, and had messengers ready to send to one another as soon as they had notice of the actual birth. Each provided for this in his own house, and the messengers of the respective parties met at an equal distance from either house, noting that neither of them could make out any difference in the position of the stars or any other minutest points. Yet Firminius, born in a high estate in his parents' house, ran his course through the more prosperous ways of this world, increased in wealth and rose to honors; whereas that slave continued to serve his masters with no relaxation of his bondage, as Firminius, who knew him, told me.

After hearing and believing these things, in view of the character of the narrator, all my resistance gave way. First, I tried to reclaim Firminius himself from that curiosity by telling him that upon inspecting his constellations, I ought, if I were to predict truly, to have seen in them parents eminent among their neighbors, a noble family in its own city, high birth, good education, liberal learning. But if that servant had consulted me upon the same constellations, since they were his also (again, if it were accurate), I would see in them a most abject lineage, a slavish condition, and everything else utterly at variance with the former. Therefore, looking at the same constellations, if I spoke the truth, I would have spoken different things to each; or if I spoke the same, I would have spoken falsely. From this it was to be gathered certainly that whatever was foretold accurately upon consideration of these constellations was determined not by art, but by chance. And whatever was foretold inaccurately wasn't from lack of skill in the art, but the error of chance.

Approaching the subject from this side, I began to consider other similar situations, so that none of those fools who followed such an occupation (whom I longed to attack and confute with ridicule), might argue against me that either Firminius had informed me falsely, or his father him. So I turned my thoughts to those who are born twins, who for the most part, emerge from the womb so close to each other that the small interval between them—however much influence they claim for it as an actual fact—can't be noted by human observation, or be accurately expressed in those figures the astrologer examines in order to predict accurately. Yet they can't be true; for looking into the same figures, he would have had to predict the same things concerning Esau and Jacob, while on the contrary the same things didn't happen to them (see Genesis 25:21–27). He must therefore have been speaking falsely. If he is to speak accurately, then looking into the same figures, he must not give the same answer.

Any accurate answer, then, isn't by art, but by chance. For you, Lord, most righteous ruler of the universe, while the consulters and the consulted don't know it, can so act upon them both by your hidden inspiration that the consulter hears out of the unsearchable depth of your righteous judgment what he ought to hear according to what his soul secretly deserves. Let no one say to you "What is this?" or "Why is that?" Let him not say it, let him not say it, for he is only a human.

And then, my Helper, you set me free from those shackles. But still I tried to find the answer to the question "Where is evil?" and found no answer. But you didn't allow me to be carried away, by any fluctuations of thought, from the faith by which I still believed both that you exist and that your substance is unchangeable, and that you care for and would judge all people, and that in Christ, your Son, our Lord, and in the Holy Scriptures, which the authority of your Church pressed upon me, you planned the way of our salvation to the life that is to come after this life, which brings death.

With these things safe and immovably settled in my mind, I eagerly attempted to find the origin of evil. What torments did my laboring heart endure! What sighs, my God! Yet even there your ears were open and I didn't know it. When in stillness I was earnestly searching, those slight expressions of regret for my misdeeds by my soul were loud appeals to your mercy. No one knew, but you alone knew what I endured. How little of it did I speak even to my closest friends! Did the total uproar of my soul, for which neither time nor words was sufficient, reach them? Yet it all went into your ears, everything that I roared out from the groanings of my heart. And my desire was before you, and the light of my eyes failed me; for that light was inside, and I was looking outside. Nor was that light in space, but my attention was directed to things contained in space.

I found no resting place, nor did external things receive me in such a way that I could say, "It's enough. All is well." Nor did they let me turn back to where it might be inferior to you. You are my true joy when I'm subjected to you, and when you've subjected to me what you created beneath me. This was the happy mean and middle way of my safety, that I should remain in your image, and by serving you, have dominion over the body.

But when I lifted myself proudly against you and "defiantly charged against the Lord, with thick, strong shields" (Job 15:26), even these inferior things were placed above me, and pressed me down, so that nowhere was there any respite or relief. Crowds and troops met my sight on all sides, and their images appeared to my thoughts unasked for as I was returning to you, as if to say to me, "Where are you going, unworthy and filthy one?" All these things had grown out of my wound, for you humble the proud like one that is wounded, and through my own inflated pride, I was separated from you. Yes, my eyes were swelled shut by my pride-bloated face.

But you, Lord, abide forever. You're not angry with us forever, because you have pity on our dust and ashes. It was pleasing in your sight to reform my deformities, and you disturbed me by inward goads to make me dissatisfied until you were revealed to my inward sight. In that way, my swelling was reduced by the secret hand of your remedy, and the disordered and darkened sight of my mind was made well from day to day by the stinging anointing of healthful sorrows.

First of all, willing to show me how you "oppose the proud but show favor to the humble" (1 Peter 5:5), and with what great mercy you've shown us the way of humility, in that your "Word became flesh and made his dwelling among us" (John 1:14), you procured for me, by means of a person puffed up with the most monstrous pride, certain books of the Platonists, translated from Greek into Latin. In them I read, not indeed the very words, but with exactly the same meaning, enforced by many and various reasonings, that "In the beginning was the Word, and the Word was with God, and the Word was God. He was with God in the beginning. Through him all things were made; without him nothing was made that has been made. In him was life, and that life was the light of all people. The light shines in the darkness, and the darkness has not overcome it." (John 1:1–4)

I also read that the human soul, though it bears witness to the light, is not itself that light. But the Word of God, being God, is "the true light that gives light to everyone." And that light "was coming into the world." And I read that "he was in the world, and though the world was made through him, the world did not recognize him." But I didn't read there that "he came to that which was his own, but his own did not receive him. Yet to all who did receive him, to those who believed in his name, he gave the right to become children of God." (John 1:9–12).

In the same way I read there that God the Word was "born not of natural descent, nor of human decision or a husband's will, but born of God." But that "the Word became flesh and made his dwelling among us" (John 1:13–14), I didn't read there.

I discovered in those books that it was said in many and different ways that the Son was in the form of the Father, and "did not consider equality with God something to be used to his own advantage," because he was naturally the same substance. I didn't read there that "he made himself nothing by taking the very nature of a servant, being made in human likeness. And being found in appearance as a human being, he humbled himself by becoming obedient to death—even death on a cross! Therefore God exalted him to the highest place and gave him the name that is above every name, that at the name of Jesus every knee should bow, in heaven and on earth and under the earth, and every tongue acknowledge that Jesus Christ is Lord, to the glory of God the Father." (Philippians 2:6–11).

I read there that before all time, and above all times, your only-begotten Son remains unchangeably co-eternal with you, and that out of "his fullness" (John 1:16) souls receive, that they may be blessed; and that by participation in the wisdom that remains in them they are renewed so that they may be wise. But I didn't read that "at just the right time . . . Christ died for the ungodly" (Romans 5:6); and that God "did not spare his own son, but gave him up for us all" (Romans 8:32).

For "you have hidden these things from the wise and learned, and revealed them to little children," so that those "who are weary and burdened" might come to him, and he will refresh them, because he is "gentle and humble in heart" (Matthew 11:25–29). And "he guides the humble in what is right and teaches them his way, looking on our affliction and our distress and taking away all our sins" (see Psalm 25:9,18).

Those who are puffed up with the elation of some would-be sublimer learning don't hear him saying, "Learn from me, for I am gentle and humble in heart, and you will find rest for your souls" (Matthew 11:29). "Although they knew God, they neither glorified him as God nor give thanks to him, but their thinking became futile and their foolish hearts were darkened. Although they claimed to be wise, they became fools" (Romans 1:21–22).

I also read there that they had "exchanged the glory of the immortal God for images made to look like mortal human beings and birds and animals and reptiles" (Romans 1:23)—namely, into the Egyptian food for which Esau lost his birthright (Genesis 25:33). The result was that your first-born people worshiped the head of a four-footed beast instead of you, turning back in heart toward Egypt, and prostrating your image (their own soul)—reducing it to extreme weakness or incapacitation, throwing themselves flat with the face down, as in submission or adoration—before "an image of a bull, which eats grass" (Psalm 106:20).

I found these things there, but I didn't feed on them. For it pleased you, Lord, to take away the reproach of his lesser status from Jacob, so that the older would serve the younger (Romans 9:12); and you've called the Gentiles into your inheritance (Ephesians 2:11–13). I had come to you from among the Gentiles, and I strained after the gold that you willed your people to take from Egypt, since wherever it was, it was yours. And to the Athenians you said by your apostle (Paul) that "in you we live and move and have our being" (see Acts 17:28), as one of their own poets had said. Certainly these books came from Athens. But I didn't set my mind on the idols of Egypt, whom they served with your gold, "exchanging the truth about God for a lie, and worshiping and serving created things rather than the Creator" (see Romans 1:25).

 Augustine catches a little—and beautiful—glimpse of God's light.

Being warned by these writers to return to myself, I entered into my inward soul, guided by you. I was able to do this because you had become my help (Psalm 30:10). I entered, and with the eye of my soul (such as it was), I saw, beyond my soul, beyond my mind, the unchangeable light. It wasn't the ordinary light that anyone can look at, nor was it, so to speak, a greater one of the same kind, as though the brightness of ordinary light were intensified many times and would fill up everything with its brilliance. This light wasn't that kind, but was far different from all these. Nor was it above my mind as oil is above water, or as heaven is above earth. It was above because it made me, and I was below it because I was made by it. Those who know the truth, know what that light is; and those who know it, know eternity. Love knows it.

Eternal truth, and true love, and beloved eternity! You are my God; to you I sigh both night and day. When I first knew you, you lifted me up, so that I might see that there was something for me to see, and that I wasn't ready to see it yet. Streaming forth your beams of light upon me most intensely, you dazzled the weakness of my sight, and I trembled with love and awe. I realized that I was far from you, in the land of unlikeness, as if I heard your voice from on high, saying, "I am the food of those who are fully grown; grow and you will feed on me. You will not change me, like the food your flesh eats, into what you are, but you will be changed into what I am."

I learned that "you rebuke and discipline people for their sins, you consume their wealth like a moth" (Psalm 39:11). I said, "Is truth, then, nothing at all, since it isn't spread out through finite or infinite space?" And you cried to me from afar, "Yes, truly 'I AM WHO I AM'" (Exodus 3:14). I heard, as the heart hears, and I had no room to doubt. I would rather have doubted that I was alive than to doubt that truth, which is "clearly seen, being understood by what has been made" (Romans 1:20).

And I viewed the other things below you, and perceived that they neither totally *are*, nor totally *are not*. They exist because they are from you; they don't exist independently, because they aren't what you are. That which truly is, is that which remains unchangeable. So "it is good" for me "to be near God" (Psalm 73:28), for if I don't remain in him, I can't remain in myself. But he, remaining in himself, renews all things. And you are the Lord my God; "apart from you I have no good thing" (Psalm 16:2).

It was made clear to me that all things that undergo corruption are (in themselves) good. If they were supremely good, they couldn't be corrupted, but neither could they be corrupted unless they were good. If they were supremely good, they would be incorruptible. If they weren't good at all, there would be nothing in them to be corrupted. For corruption injures, but unless it could diminish goodness, it couldn't harm. So then, either corruption doesn't injure (which can't be the case), or, what is most certain of all, all that is corrupted is deprived of some good.

A turning point: Augustine realizes that, although something created is "corruptible," because it's made by God it can be altogether good!

But if things that are corrupted are deprived of all good, they will cease to exist. For if they could exist, and now can be no longer corrupted, they would be better than before, because they would remain incorruptible. What could be more monstrous than to affirm that things are made better by losing all their goodness? Therefore, if they were deprived of all good, they would no longer exist. Then so long as they exist, they are good. Therefore, whatever is, is good.

Evil then, the origin of which I tried to find, is not a substance at all. For if it were a substance, it would be good. For either it would be an incorruptible substance, and so a chief good, or a corruptible substance, which couldn't be corrupted unless it were good. I perceived therefore, and it was shown to me, that you made all things good, and that there is no substance at all that you didn't make. And it's because you haven't made all things equal that each individual thing is called good, and all things together are called not only good, but very good, for our "God saw all that he had made, and it was very good" (Genesis 1:31).

To you evil is nothing at all. Not only to you, but also to your creation as a whole, there is nothing outside that could break in and mar the order that you've appointed for it. But in the parts of it, some things, because they aren't in harmony with others, are considered evil. Yet those same things harmonize with others and are good, and in themselves are good. All these things that don't harmonize together, still harmonize with the lower part of creation that we call the earth, which has its own cloudy and windy sky harmonizing with it.

Far be it from me, then, to say, "These things shouldn't be." For if I saw nothing but these, I would indeed long for better; but even for these alone I would praise you, for that you are to be praised is shown by that fact that "from the earth, great sea creatures and all ocean depths, lightning and hail, snow and clouds, stormy winds that do your bidding. Mountains and all hills, fruit trees and all cedars, wild animals and all cattle, small creatures and flying birds, kings of the earth and all nations, princes and all rulers on earth, young men and women, old men and children"—all these praise your name! (See Psalm 148:7–12.) And "from the heavens, our God, all your angels praise you in the heights above, and all your heavenly hosts, sun and moon, all shining stars, the highest heavens, and the waters above the skies"—all these praise your name. (See Psalm 148:1–5.) Now I didn't long for better things, because I considered them all, and with a sounder judgment I realized that while the things above were better than those below, all things together were better than those above would be by themselves alone.

There is no wholeness in those who are displeased with any part of your creation, no more than there was in me when I was displeased with so many things that you had made. Because my soul didn't dare to be displeased with my God, I preferred not to consider that which displeased me as yours. I had accepted the notion of two substances (one evil, one good), and I found no rest, but kept talking idly.

Turning from that error, I made for myself a god that occupied infinite measures of all space, and thought that it was you, and placed the god in my heart. But again, it had become the temple of its own idol, and an abomination to you. But after you had eased the pain of my mind, unknown to me, and closed my eyes so that they shouldn't observe emptiness, I let up on myself a little, and my madness was lulled to sleep. I awoke in you, and saw you to be infinite in a different way; but that sight didn't come from the flesh.

I looked back at other things, and I saw that they owed their being to you; and were all bounded in you; but in a different way, not as being in space, but because you contain all things in the hand of your truth. All things are true insofar as they have being. There is no falsehood, unless what doesn't exist is thought to exist. I saw that all things harmonized, not only with their places, but with their seasons. And that you, who alone are eternal, didn't begin to work after innumerable eons of time had passed, because all periods of time, past and future, neither come to pass nor pass away, except through your working and abiding.

I understood, and had thought nothing of it, that the same bread that's distasteful to a sick palate is pleasant to a healthy one, and that light is offensive to sore eyes, but delightful to sound ones. Your righteousness displeases the wicked; but so do the vipers and smaller worms. Yet you created these creatures good, giving them a suitable place in the lower parts of your creation. The wicked themselves are well suited there, and even more so, the more unlike you they become. They fit in with the higher creatures as they become more like you. I asked what iniquity—gross immorality—was, and found that it wasn't a substance at all, but the perversion of the will, which has turned away from you, God, the Supreme Substance, toward these lower things, and has thrown away its inner self and has swelled up outwardly.

 This is a major theological point for Augustine, and it's considered one of his primary contributions to Christian theology: evil, or sin, isn't an issue of substances that

have gone wrong; instead, it's a problem of the human
will that has (will-fully) turned against God.

And I wondered if I now loved you or an imaginary fantasy instead of you. I didn't deserve to enjoy my God, but I was transported to you by your beauty, and was soon torn away from you by my own weight, sinking with sorrow into the lower things. This weight was fleshly habit. Yet there remained with me a remembrance of you, and I didn't doubt at all that there was One to whom I might cling faithfully. But I felt that I was not yet one who could cling faithfully to you. For the corrupted body presses down the soul, and the earthly dwelling weighs down the mind that thinks upon many things.

I was most sure that "since the creation of the world your invisible qualities—your eternal power and divine nature—have been clearly seen, being understood from what has been made" (Romans 1:20). Examining the origin of my admiration for the beauty of the heavenly and earthly bodies, I attempted to understand what aided me in making correct judgments, when I did make them. I was now touching on the unchangeable and true eternity of truth, above my changeable mind.

And so by degrees, I passed from physical bodies to the soul that perceives them through the bodily senses, and then to its inward faculty to which the bodily senses report outward things. The faculties of animals reach this far. And from there, again I passed on to the faculty of reason, to which whatever is received from the senses of the body is referred for judgment. This reasoning faculty, finding itself to be a changeable thing in me, aroused itself to the limit of its own understanding and led my thoughts away from the tyranny of habit.

My reason withdrew from the multitudes of contradictory mental images so that it might discover what that light was with which it was being bathed. Then, without a shadow of doubt, it cried out that "the unchangeable was to be preferred to the changeable." And from that it recognized and acknowledged the unchangeable, because unless it recognized and acknowledged the unchangeable, it could have had no sure ground to prefer it to the changeable. With the flash of one trembling glance, it arrived at That Which Is. And then I saw that your "invisible qualities have been clearly seen from what has been made" (Romans 1:20). But I couldn't steady my gaze on this revelation. My frailty and weakness were beaten back again, and I returned again to my old habits, taking along with me only a loving memory of this insight, and a longing for what I had, so to speak, caught the fragrance of, but as yet wasn't able to eat.

Then I looked for a way to obtain enough strength to enjoy you, but didn't find it until I embraced that "Mediator between God and human beings, Christ Jesus, himself human, who is God over all, forever praised!" (1 Timothy 2:5, Romans 9:5). He was calling to me, saying, "I am the way and the truth and the life" (John 14:6), mingling flesh with the food that I was unable to receive. For "the Word became flesh" (John 1:14), so that your wisdom by which you created all things might provide milk for our infant state.

I didn't know Jesus to be my God. Though humbled, I didn't yet grasp the humble One, nor did I yet recognize what his weakness was designed to teach. For your Word, the eternal truth, who is exalted above your highest creatures, raises up those who are subject to himself. In this lower world, he built for himself a lowly habitation made from our clay, by which he intended to bring down from themselves those who would be subjected to him. He intended to bring them over to himself, reducing their swollen pride and increasing their love, so that they might go on no further in self-confidence but rather consent to become weak, seeing the Deity before their feet, become weak by taking on our mortality. It was his intent that they, seeing themselves to be worn out, might cast themselves down on him, so that rising again, he might lift them up.

Here we see Augustine's first acknowledgment that Jesus Christ, though he ate, slept, drank, and walked like other "corruptible" things, was in fact God.

But I thought differently, thinking only of my Lord Christ as being a man of excellent wisdom to whom no one could be compared. Being miraculously born of a virgin, he seemed to have attained his great height of authority in this way, to be an example of despising temporal things to obtain immortality, through God's care for us. But what mystery there was in the Word made flesh, I couldn't even imagine. This I had learned from what is delivered to us in Scripture about him, however, that he ate, drank, slept, walked, was glad in spirit, was sorrowful, and preached.

Flesh alone didn't adhere to your Word except with a human soul and mind. All who know the unchangeableness of your Word know this. I now knew this as well as I could, and I didn't doubt it at all.

To move the limbs of the body by will at one time, and at another to remain still; at one moment to be moved by some emotion, at another not; to deliver wise sayings through human speech, then to keep silence—all these belong to the soul and mind, which are subject to change. And if these things were falsely written about him, all the rest would be in danger of being labeled false. Nothing would remain in those Scriptures that could have any saving faith for humankind. But since they were written truthfully, I acknowledged Christ to be a perfect and complete man—not the body of a man only, nor only a feeling soul without a rational one with the body as well, but true man. This very man was to be preferred above all others, not only as being a form of truth, but because of the great excellence of his human nature and his more perfect participation in the divine wisdom.

But Alypius thought Christians believed God to be so clothed with flesh that there was no soul at all in Christ, and he didn't think that a human mind was ascribed to him. And because he was fully persuaded that the actions recorded about him could have been performed only by a vital and rational creature, he moved more slowly toward the Christian faith. Understanding afterward that this was the error of the Apollinarian heretics, he was filled with joy in the Christian faith and accepted it.

The early church wrestled with many heresies (false teachings) as it defined what became known as the true faith. Augustine is referring here to Apollinaris of Laodicea, who taught errors in the fourth century that were condemned by the Church.

But I admit that it was only some time later that I learned how in that sentence, "The Word became flesh" (John 1:14), catholic doctrine is distinguished from the falsehood of Photinus. For the rejection of the truth by heretics makes the tenets of your Church and sound doctrine stand out more clearly. "No doubt there have to be differences among you to show which of you have God's approval" (1 Corinthians 11:19).

Having read the books of the Platonists and having been taught by them to search for the truth that stands outside of the physical realm, I saw that "your invisible qualities are understood from what has been made" (Romans 1:20). And though I was foiled in this attempt to attain to the nonphysical truth, I perceived what the truth was that the darkness of my mind would not permit me to contemplate. I was sure that you exist, and that you are infinite, yet not diffused in space, finite or infinite; that you truly are the same forever, varying neither in any part nor by any motion; and that all other things spring from you, as is proved by the fact that they exist at all.

I was sure of these things, yet I was too weak in faith to enjoy you. I chattered like one well skilled; but if I hadn't attempted to find your way in Christ our Savior, I would have proved to be not skilled, but killed. For now, filled with my own punishment, I had begun to wish to appear wise. Yet I didn't grieve, but rather was puffed up with knowledge.

Where was the charity that builds upon the foundation of humility, which is Christ Jesus? Or when would the books of the philosophers teach me that? I believe you willed that I should become acquainted with them before I studied your Scriptures, so that it might be imprinted on my memory how they affected me.

 Augustine recognizes that God allowed him to search for the truth in books of philosophy so that when he later found God's truth in the Scriptures he would appreciate it all the more.

And you willed that afterward, having been subdued through your books, and my wounds having been touched by your healing fingers, I might discern and distinguish the difference between presumption and confession, between those on the one hand who see where they are to go, yet don't see the way, and on the other, the way that leads us not only to observe the home of exalted joy and blessedness, but to dwell in it. For if I had first been formed in your Holy Scriptures, and if you had grown sweet to me in the familiar use of them, and if I had then fallen upon these other volumes, they might have led me away from the solid ground of true devotion and reverence. Or if I had stood firm in the wholesome disposition that I had gained from Scripture, I might have thought it could also have been obtained from the study of those books alone.

Most eagerly, then, I seized that venerable writing of your Spirit, and especially upon the apostle Paul. Those difficulties vanished away in which he at one time seemed to me to contradict himself, and the text of his discourse had seemed not to agree with the testimonies of the Law and the Prophets. That pure Word now seemed to me to have only one face, and I learned to be glad with trembling.

So I began, and I found that whatever truth I had read in those other books was declared here amid the praises of your grace, so that whoever sees it wouldn't boast as though they hadn't received, not only *what* they see, but also the *power of seeing,* for "what do you have that you have not received?" (1 Corinthians 4:7). And I found that not only may they be taught to see you, who are ever the same, but also, being healed, they may take hold of you. And I found that those who can't see you from afar, may still walk on the way by which they may reach, observe, and possess you. For "I delight in God's law; but I see another law at work in me, waging war against the law of my mind and making me a prisoner of the law of sin at work within me" (Romans 7:22-23). For "Lord, you are righteous," but "we have sinned and done wrong" (Daniel 9:7, 5). Your hand has grown heavy upon us, and we are justly delivered over to that ancient sinner, the governor of death, who persuaded our will to be like his will, whereby he didn't hold to your truth (John 8:44).

What shall we wretched mortals do? "Who will rescue me from this body of death?" Only your grace, "through Jesus Christ our Lord" (Romans 7:24), whom you've begotten co-eternal with you and formed "before your deeds of old" (Proverbs 8:22). The prince of this world (John 14:30) found nothing in him worthy of death. Yet he killed him, and "the charge of legal indebtedness, which stood against us and condemned us," was "canceled" (Colossians 2:14).

The Platonic writings didn't contain this. Their pages don't express this kind of devotion and reverence—the tears of confession, your sacrifice, a troubled spirit, "a broken and contrite heart" (Psalm 51:17), the salvation of your people, the Holy City prepared as a bride beautifully dressed for her husband, the promise of the Holy Spirit, the cup of our redemption. No one sings there, "Truly my soul finds rest in God; my salvation comes from him. Truly he is my rock and my salvation; he is my fortress, I will never be shaken" (Psalm 62:1-2). No one there hears him calling, "Come to me, all you who are weary and burdened." They sneer at learning from him, because he is "gentle and humble in heart," and "because you have hidden these things from the wise and learned, and revealed them to little children" (Matthew 11:28-29, 25).

It's one thing, from the wooded mountaintop to view the land of peace, and fail to find the way to it—to attempt impassible ways in vain, beset by fugitives and deserters and opposed by their captain, the lion and the dragon. It's quite another thing to keep on the way that leads there, guarded by the hosts of the heavenly King, where those who have deserted the heavenly army can't rob us—indeed they recoil from the way as torment itself. These things sank wonderfully into my heart when I read "the least" of your apostles [as the apostle Paul called himself in 1 Corinthians 15:9], and meditated upon your works, and trembled.

Chapter Eight

Conversion

My God, let me remember and confess with gratitude to you your mercies over me. Let my bones be steeped in your love, and let them say to you, "Who is like you, LORD?" (Psalm 35:10) "You have loosed my bonds of affliction. I will sacrifice a thank offering to you" (Psalm 115:16-17). I will declare how you have crushed my bones (Psalm 51:8). And all who worship you, when they hear these things, will say, "Praise be to his glorious name forever; may the whole earth be filled with his glory" (Psalm 72:19).

Your words had fastened themselves in my heart, and I was surrounded by you on all sides. I was certain of your eternal life, though I had seen it as "only a reflection as in a mirror" (1 Corinthians 13:12). I no longer doubted that there was an incorruptible substance from which all other substance came. I no longer desired to be more certain of you, but to be more steadfast in you.

As for my temporal life, all things were wavering, and my heart had to be purged from the old yeast (1 Corinthians 5:7). The way, and the Savior himself, pleased me greatly, but I still shrank from going through the narrowness of that way. Then you put into my mind, and it seemed good to me, to go to Simplicianus, who seemed to me a faithful servant of yours. Your grace shone in him. I had heard also that beginning in his youth he had lived in complete devotion to you. Now he was advanced in years, and because of his great age—spent in such zeal in following your ways—I thought it likely that he had learned much from his experience, and so he had. Out of that store of experience I hoped that he would advise me, as I set my anxieties before him, about what would be the most appropriate way, for one as afflicted as I was, to walk in your paths.

 He realizes that he needs the advice of an older person— Simplicianus—someone wiser than himself.

I saw that the church was full, with one going this way, and another that. But I wasn't happy to lead a secular life. Since my hopes of honor and wealth no longer spurred me on, it was a very grievous burden to tolerate so heavy a state of subjection. Compared to your sweetness and the beauty of your house, which I loved, those things no longer delighted me.

But I was still tenaciously gripped by the love of women. Now, the apostle Paul didn't forbid me to marry, although he exhorted me to something better, wishing everyone to be unmarried as he was.

But, being weak, I chose the more indulgent place. And because of this alone, I was tossed up and down in indecision, faint and wasted with numbing cares, because I would be inhibited in other matters contrary to my desires if I obligated myself to undertake a married life, to which I was so completely bound. I had heard from the mouth of truth that some "have renounced marriage because of the kingdom of heaven. The one who can accept this should accept it" (Matthew 19:12).

Surely all people "who were ignorant of God were foolish by nature; and they were unable from the good things that are seen to know him who exists" (Wisdom 13:1 RSV). But I was no longer in that vanity; I had surmounted it, and by the united witness of your whole creation had found you, our Creator, and your Word—God with you—by whom you created all things (John 1:1–3).

But there is another kind of lack of reverence, that of people who when "they knew God, they neither glorified him as God nor gave thanks to him" (Romans 1:21). I had fallen into this, but "your right hand sustained me" (Psalm 18:35), and took me from it, and you placed me where I could recover. For you've said to humankind, "The fear of the Lord—that is wisdom" (Job 28:28), and again, "Answer fools according to their folly, or they will be wise in their own eyes" (Proverbs 26:5). "Although they claimed to be wise, they became fools" (Romans 1:22). But now I had found the pearl of great value, which I ought to have sold all I had and bought (Matthew 13:45). But I hesitated.

I went to Simplicianus, then, the spiritual father of Ambrose (at that time bishop of Milan), who loved him as truly as a father. I told him the story of my wanderings. But when I mentioned that I had read certain books of the Platonists, which had been translated into Latin by Victorinus, formerly professor of rhetoric at Rome (who died a Christian, as I had been told), Simplicianus expressed his joy that I hadn't come across the writings of other philosophers, which were full of fallacies and deceits, "depending on human tradition" (Colossians 2:8). The Platonists, on the other hand, in many ways led to belief in God and his Word.

Then to exhort me to the humility of Christ, "hidden from the wise and learned and revealed to little children" (Matthew 11:25), he spoke about Victorinus himself, whom he had known most intimately while he was at Rome. I won't hold back what he told me about him, for it contains great praise of your grace which ought to be acknowledged to you.

 Here we have the story of Victorinus' conversion, which Augustine uses to foreshadow his own.

He told me that Victorinus had been highly skilled in the liberal arts, had read many philosophical writings, had read them with discernment, and had been the teacher of many noble senators. As a memorial of his distinction as a teacher, a statue of him had been placed in the Roman Forum (something that persons of this world esteem a high honor). Up to that time he had been a worshiper of idols and a participant in the sacrilegious rites to which almost all the nobility of Rome were given. He had inspired the people in their love of

> The barking deity, Anubis, and all the motley crew
> Of monster gods who stood in arms 'gainst Neptune,
> Venus, Minerva, and the steel-clad Mars.
> (Virgil's Aeneid)

Rome had once conquered these gods but now worshiped them [that is, having defeating the Greeks in battle, the Romans adopted Greek mythology], and all this the aged Victorinus had defended with thundering eloquence for many years. But now he didn't blush to be the child of your Christ, a new-born babe at your baptismal font, bowing his neck to the yoke of humility, and subduing his pride to the reproach of the cross (1 Corinthians 1:18–21).

Lord, Lord, "who parted the heavens and came down," who "touched the mountains, so that they smoked" (Psalm 146:5), by what means did you convey yourself to that heart? Victorinus used to read the Holy Scriptures, as Simplicianus said, and most studiously searched into all the Christian writings. To Simplicianus he said, not openly, but privately, as to a friend, "Please understand that I'm already a Christian." Simplicianus answered, "I won't believe it, nor will I rank you among Christians, until I see you in Christ's church." The other replied teasingly, "Then do walls make Christians?" And he often repeated that he was already a Christian. But Simplicianus just as often made the same answer, and the joke about "walls" was repeated by the other again. For he was fearful of offending his friends, proud demon-worshipers, fearing a storm of enmity might fall heavily on him from the height of their Babylonian dignity, as from cedars of Lebanon, which the Lord had not yet broken down (Psalm 29:5).

But when he had gathered strength by reading and diligent inquiry, he began to be afraid of being denied by Christ before the holy angels if now he would be afraid to acknowledge him before men (Luke 12:9). He began to feel himself guilty of a great offense in being ashamed of the sacraments of the humility of your work, when he had not been ashamed of the sacrilegious rites of those proud demons, whose pride he had imitated and whose rites he had adopted. He became shame-faced against the emptiness of those rites and bold-faced toward the truth.

Suddenly and unexpectedly, he said to Simplicianus, as he told me, "Let's go to the church, because I want to become a Christian." Simplicianus, unable to contain himself for joy, went with him. And having been admitted to the first sacramental instructions and having become a catechumen, not long afterward he gave his name as a candidate for regeneration by baptism, to the wonder of Rome and the joy of the Church. The proud "saw and were vexed, they gnashed their teeth and wasted away" (Psalm 112:10)! But the Lord God was the hope of your servant, and he didn't "look to the proud, to those who turn aside to false gods" (Psalm 40:4).

Finally, the hour came to make his profession of faith. At Rome, those who are about to come to your grace deliver a set of words, committed to memory, from an elevated place in the sight of all the faithful. The presbyters offered Victorinus the chance to make his profession more privately. This was often done to those who were likely to be put off by their timidity. But Victorinus chose rather to profess his salvation openly, stating that he had taught rhetoric and had publicly professed it, yet there was no salvation in it. How much less then should he dread your humble flock when proclaiming your word, when he had not feared a frenzied multitude of pagans when proclaiming his own words!

So then, when he went up to make his profession, everyone, as they recognized him, whispered his name to one another, with the voice of congratulations. And who was there who didn't know him? A low murmur ran through all the mouths of the rejoicing multitude, "Victorinus! Victorinus!" The sudden burst of rapture at the sight of him was followed by a sudden hush so that everyone could hear him. He proclaimed the true faith with great boldness, and they all desired to hold him in their hearts. Indeed, they took him into their hearts in their love and joy and received him with warm handshakes and embraces.

Good God, what takes place in us that we rejoice more at the salvation of a soul whom we had despaired of and who was freed from greater peril, than if there had always been hope for him, or if the danger had been less? For you also, merciful Father, rejoice more "over one sinner who repents than over ninety-nine righteous persons who do not need to repent" (Luke 15:7). And with much joyfulness we hear about the sheep that has strayed and is brought back upon the shepherd's shoulders while the angels rejoice (Luke 15:6), and how the coin is restored to your treasury while the neighbors rejoice with the woman who found it (Luke 15:9). And the joy of the solemn service of your house brings tears to our eyes when we hear the story of your younger [prodigal] son, that he "was dead, and is alive again; he was lost and is found" (Luke 15:32). You rejoice in us and in your holy angels, holy through holy love. You're always the same, and in the same way you know all things that don't remain the same and are not eternal.

What, then, goes on in the soul when it's more delighted at finding or recovering the things it loves, than if they had never been lost? Yes, and other things witness to the same thing, and there are many things that bear witness to this reality, and they all cry out, "Yes, this is true." The conquering

commander triumphs; yet he wouldn't have conquered if he hadn't fought; and the greater the
danger there was in the battle, the more joy there is
in the triumph. The storm tosses the sailors,
threatens shipwreck, and every one grows pale with
the threat of death; the sky and sea become calm and
they celebrate as intensely as they had been afraid. A
sick friend's pulse indicates danger; everyone who
wants them to get well is sick at heart over them.
They recover, though not as yet able to walk with
their former strength; yet there is more joy than
there was earlier, when they walked sound and
strong.

Yes, it's through difficulties that we acquire the
very pleasures of human life—not only the difficulties that rush upon us unexpectedly and against
our wills, but those that are voluntary and planned.
There's no pleasure in eating and drinking unless
the pinching of hunger and thirst go before.
Drunkards eat certain salty meats to create a painful
thirst, and the drink brings pleasure as it relieves it.
It's also customary that the promised bride not be
given too quickly, so that the husband will not have
less esteem for the woman whom as his fiancée he
had longed for.

This law holds true both in base and dishonorable
pleasures and in the pleasures that are permitted and
lawful: in the sincerity of honest friendship, in the
person who was dead and was alive again, in the
sheep or the coin that had been lost and was found.
Everywhere the greater joy is ushered in by the

greater pain. What does this mean, Lord my God, when you're an everlasting joy to your own Self, and some things about you are ever rejoicing in you? What does it mean that this portion of creation ebbs and flows this way, alternating between displeasing you and being reconciled to you? Is this their allotted measure? Is this all you've assigned to them, that from the highest heavens to the lowest depth of earth, from the beginning of the world to the end of the ages, from the angel to the worm, from the first motion to the last, you set each in its place and appoint each in its proper season—everything good in its own way?

You're the highest of the high, and I'm among the lowest of the low! You never depart from us, and yet we—how hard it is for us to return to you!

Arise, Lord, and act! Stir us up, and recall us; kindle and draw us; stir us to passionate feeling, grow sweet to us; let us love you, let us run after you.

Don't many people return to you out of a deeper hell of blindness than Victorinus? Those who approach and are enlightened by you, receive power from you to become your children (John 1:12). But even though they are less well known than Victorinus, those who know them are glad for them. Yet when many people rejoice together, the joy of each is fuller, being kindled and stirred by one another. But because those who are widely known influence many toward salvation, and lead the way for many to follow, those who went before them rejoice greatly in them, because they don't rejoice over them alone [but also for all who will be positively influenced by them].

Let it never be that in your tabernacle the presence of the rich should be more welcome than that of the poor, or the noble more than the humble; seeing rather that you have chosen "the weak things of the world to shame the strong, . . . the lowly things of this world and the despised things—and the things that are not—to nullify the things that are" (1 Corinthians 1:27-28). And it was "the least" of your apostles (1 Corinthians 15:9), by whose tongue you sounded forth these words. Yet when Paulus the proconsul, his pride conquered by the apostle's words, was made to pass under the easy yoke of your Christ and became a provincial governor of the great king (that is, becoming God's representative), this apostle was pleased to be called Paul instead of his former name, Saul, in testimony of so great a victory.

 The story of the conversion of Sergius Paulus is told in Acts, chapter thirteen.

For there is a greater victory over an enemy when he is defeated in one in whom he has more hold and by whom he has hold of more people. But he has more hold of the proud through their concern about position, and through them, he controls more people by their authority.

Therefore, the more the heart of Victorinus was esteemed by the world, something the devil had held as an impregnable possession, and the greater the value set on his tongue—the mighty and keen weapon he had used to defeat so many, so much more should your children be glad, seeing that our king had tied up the strong man (Matthew 12:29). They saw his weapons taken from him and cleansed, and made fit for your honor, and made "useful to the Master and prepared to do any good work" (2 Timothy 2:21).

Now when that man of yours, Simplicianus, told me about Victorinus, I burned with eagerness to imitate him. It was for this very purpose that he related the story to me. But when he had added, also, that in the days of the Emperor Julian, a law was made forbidding Christians to teach literature and rhetoric, and that Victorinus, in obedience to this law, chose to abandon the school of worthless language rather than your word, by which you "opened the mouth of the dumb, and made the tongues of babes speak clearly" (Wisdom 10:21 RSV), he appeared to me not only brave but happy, having found in this way an opportunity to serve you alone.

This was the very thing I was hoping for, bound as I was, not by the irons of another person, but by my own iron will.

 Augustine describes his last moments of struggle against Christianity: now it was a matter of will.

The enemy held my will, and by it had made a chain and bound me. For from a perverse will comes lust; and lust yielded to, becomes habit; and habit not resisted, becomes necessity. By these links, joined together as in a chain, a hard bondage held me in slavery. But that new will that had begun to develop in me, to serve you freely and to wish to enjoy you, my God, my only certain joy, wasn't yet able to overcome my former long-established willfulness. Therefore my two wills, the new and the old, the physical and the spiritual, struggled within me, and by their confrontation, undid my soul.

I came to understand through my own experience what I had read, that "the sinful nature desires what is contrary to the Spirit, and the Spirit what is contrary to the sinful nature" (Galatians 5:17). I experienced both; but now I was experiencing more of what I approved of in myself than of what I disapproved of. For concerning the latter, it was now "no longer I myself who did it" (Romans 7:17), because in much of it I remained passive and reluctant. Yet it was by my own action that this habit had gained such power of warring against me. I had come willingly to the place that I now wanted not to be in. And who has any right to speak against it, when just punishment follows the sinner? Nor did I any longer have my former excuse, that I was still hesitating to turn my back on the world and serve you because I wasn't altogether certain of the truth. By now I was indeed certain. But, still in slavery to the earth, I refused to be your soldier, and was as much afraid to be freed of all the encumbrances as I ought to have been afraid to be weighed down with them.

I was held down with the baggage of this world as pleasurably as one often is when sleeping. The thoughts in which I meditated on you were like the efforts of a person who wants to wake up, yet is still overcome with heavy drowsiness and falls asleep again. No one wants to sleep forever, and sober judgment says that waking is better. Yet a sleepy person, for the most part, feeling that heavy lethargy in all their limbs, often delays shaking off sleep, and though half-displeased with themselves, still, even after it's time to get up, yields to it with pleasure.

In the same way I was assured that it would be much better for me to give myself up to your charity than to yield myself to my own lust. Though the former course satisfied and convinced me, the latter still pleased me and held me in chains. I had no answer to you when you called me: "Wake up, sleeper, rise from the dead, and Christ will shine on you" (Ephesians 5:14). When you showed me on all sides that what you said was true, and I was convicted by the truth, I had nothing at all to answer. All I could say were those dull and drowsy words, "Soon, soon; leave me for a little while."

But "soon, soon" had no present, and my "little while" went on for a long while. It was in vain that "in my inner being I delighted in your law"; while "I saw another law at work in me, waging war against the law of my mind and making me a prisoner of the law of sin at work within me" (Romans 7:22-23). The law of sin is in the violence of habit, by which the mind is drawn and held, even against its will. Yet it deserves this, because it willingly fell into it. Who then would "rescue me from this body of death," but your grace alone, "through Jesus Christ our Lord" (Romans 7:24-25).

And now I will declare and confess your name, Lord, my helper and redeemer, how you delivered me out of the bonds of sexual desire by which I was bound most firmly, and out of slavery to worldly things. Amid increasing anxiety I was doing my usual business, and sighing to you every day. I attended church whenever I was free from the business under the burden of which I groaned. Alypius was with me, now free from his legal office after his third term as assessor, and awaiting clients to whom to sell his counsel, as I sold the skill of speaking (if indeed teaching can impart it).

To please us, Nebridius had consented to teach under Verecundus, a citizen and a grammarian of Milan and an intimate friend of us all, who had urgently requested and by right of friendship challenged from our group the faithful aid he needed. Nebridius wasn't drawn to do this by any desire of gain, for he might have made much more from his education if he had chosen to, but as a most kind and gentle friend he wouldn't let our request go unanswered. He did this all very discreetly, taking care not to become known to those people whom the world considered great. He avoided distraction of mind, wanting to leave himself free to search for, or read, or hear something concerning wisdom.

One day, when Nebridius was away—for some reason I can't recall—a man named Ponticianus came to see Alypius and me. He was an African who held high office in the emperor's court. What he wanted of us I don't know, but we sat down to converse, and he observed a book on the table. He opened it, and to his surprise found it to be the epistles of the apostle Paul.

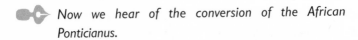

Now we hear of the conversion of the African Ponticianus.

He had thought it would be one of those books that I was wearing myself out teaching. Looking at me with a smile, he expressed his joy and wonder that he had suddenly found this book, and only this one, before my eyes. For he was a baptized Christian, and often bowed himself before you, our God, in church, in constant and daily prayer.

When I told him that I studied these Scriptures with much care, we fell into conversation about Antony, the Egyptian monk, whose name was held in high regard by your people, though up to that time not familiar to us. When he learned this, he dwelt more on that subject, amazed that we didn't know about one so famous. We also were amazed, hearing of your wonderful works done in the true faith of the Church, in times so recent—almost in our own—and so fully documented. We all wondered—we that they were so great, and he, that we knew nothing about them.

His conversation turned to the large numbers in the monasteries, and their holy ways, a sweet smelling savor to you, and of the fruitful deserts of the wilderness, of which we knew nothing. There was a monastery at Milan, full of good brothers, just outside the city walls, under the protection of Ambrose, but we didn't know it. He went on with his talk, and we listened intently and in silence.

He then told us how one afternoon at Trier, when the Emperor was taken up with the circus games, He [Ponticianus] and three friends went out to walk in gardens near the city walls. There, as they happened to walk in pairs, one of them went apart with him, while the other two wandered by themselves; these, in their wanderings came on a certain cottage inhabited by some of your servants, poor in spirit, of whom is the kingdom of heaven (Matthew 5:3), and there they found a little book containing the life of Antony. One of them began to read it and admire it, and was stirred to action by it.

As he read, he began to consider taking up such a life and giving up his worldly service to serve you. He and his companion were two of those they call "agents for public affairs." Suddenly filled with holy love and a sober sense of shame, angry with himself, he looked at his friend and said, "Tell me, please, what do we gain by all these labors of ours? What are we aiming at? What do we serve? Can our hopes in court rise higher than to be emperor's favorites? And in such a position, what is there that isn't fragile and full of dangers? By how many perils will we arrive at even greater peril? When will we arrive there? If I desire to become a friend of God, I can do so at once!" That's what he said. And in the labor pangs of new life, he turned his eyes again on the book and read on, and was inwardly changed.

His mind was separated from the world, as soon became evident. As he read, and the waves of his heart rolled up and down, he stormed at himself for a while. Then he saw and resolved on a better course, and now having become yours, he said to his friend, "Now I have broken loose from those false hopes, and am determined to serve God. From this hour, in this place, I enter that service. If you won't imitate me, don't oppose me." His friend answered that he would stick with him, to participate in so glorious a reward, so glorious a service. So both of them, now being yours, were building a tower at the necessary cost (Luke 14:28)—forsaking all they had and following you.

Then Ponticianus and the friend who was with him, who had been walking in other parts of the garden, came in search of them to the same place. On finding them, they reminded them to return, as the day was declining. But the others, relating their resolution and purpose and how the resolve had begun and had become confirmed in them, begged them not to stop them if they wouldn't join them. Ponticianus and his friend, though not changed from their former state, nevertheless (as he told us) expressed sorrow over themselves and earnestly and devoutly congratulated their friends and commended themselves to their prayers. So with hearts lingering on the earth, they went away to the palace. But the other two, fixing their hearts on heaven, remained in the cottage. Both of them were engaged to be married. The women they were engaged to, when they heard of this, also dedicated their virginity to you.

Such was the story of Ponticianus. You, Lord, were focusing it on me while he was speaking, taking me from behind my own back, where I had placed myself, being unwilling to look at myself. You set me before my own face so that I might see how foul I was, how crooked and sordid, how spotted and ulcerous. I observed and loathed myself, but I could find nowhere to flee from myself. If I tried to turn my eyes from myself, Ponticianus went on with his story, and again you set me face to face with myself and thrust me before my eyes, so that I might discover my gross immorality and hate it. I knew it, but acted as though I didn't see it— winked at it and forgot it.

The more fervently I loved those whose wholesome affections I heard about, men who had given themselves up wholly to you to be healed, the more I detested myself compared to them. For many years (perhaps twelve) had gone by since my nineteenth year, when I was stirred to an earnest love of wisdom on reading Cicero's *Hortensius*. Yet I was still delaying to reject worldly happiness to devote myself to search out that of which not only the finding, but the very search itself was preferable to the treasures and kingdoms of this world.

Here's a famous (and funny) line: "Give me chastity... but not yet!"

I, a miserable young man, most miserable, even in the very earliest days of my youth, had prayed to you for chastity in this way: "Give me chastity and abstinence from sexual activity, but not yet." I was afraid that you would hear me too soon and deliver me from the disease of lust that I wished to have satisfied rather than extinguished. And I had wandered through crooked ways in a sacrilegious superstition, not indeed sure of it, but preferring it to the truth that I didn't religiously try to find, but rather maliciously opposed.

I had thought that I delayed rejecting my worldly hopes from day to day and following only you, because there didn't appear any sure way by which to direct my course. But now the day had come in which I was to be laid bare to myself and my conscience was to scold me. "Where are you now, my tongue? You said that you didn't like to cast off the baggage of emptiness for uncertain truth. Now truth is certain, yet that burden still oppresses you, while those who have neither worn themselves out with searching for it, nor for ten years and more have been thinking about it, have had their shoulders unburdened and received wings to fly away."

I was inwardly consumed and confused with horrible shame while Ponticianus was speaking. Having finished his tale and the business he came for, he went his way. And I went into myself. What did I say that wasn't against myself? With what whips of condemnation did I not lash my soul, that it might follow me, striving to go after you! Yet it drew back; it refused, and it didn't excuse itself. All arguments were exhausted and confuted. There remained a silent shrinking away. My soul was afraid as it would be afraid of death, to be restrained from the continuation of that habit by which it was actually wasting away to death.

In the midst of this great battle in my heart that I had strongly raised up against my soul, troubled in mind and countenance, I turned upon Alypius. "What is wrong with us?" I exclaimed. "What is it? What did you hear? Uneducated people start up and take heaven by force; and we, with all our education, but lacking heart, wallow in flesh and blood! Are we ashamed to follow because others have gone before us, and not ashamed instead that we aren't following?"

I uttered words such as these, and in my excitement, I flung myself away from him, while he stood looking at me in astonished silence. It wasn't my usual tone, and my forehead, my cheeks, eyes, color, the tone of my voice—all expressed my emotion more than words.

A little garden lay outside our lodging, which we had the use of, as we did of the whole house, for the owner of the house, our landlord, wasn't living there. The tempestuous agitation of my heart drove me there, where no person might interfere with the raging inner battle in which I had become engaged. How it would end, you knew, but I didn't. I was crazy to be whole and dying to live, knowing what an evil thing I was, and not knowing what good thing I was shortly to become. I retired then to the garden, with Alypius on my steps. His presence wasn't a bar to my privacy. How could he forsake me when I was in such a state? We sat down as far away from the house as possible.

I was troubled in spirit, vehemently angry with myself that I hadn't entered your will and covenant, my God. All my bones cried out to me to enter, praising it to the skies. We don't enter that place by ships or chariots or feet, not even by going as far as I had come from the house to where we were sitting. For not only to go, but to enter your will was nothing else but to will to enter, resolutely and completely—not to swagger and sway about with a changeable and half-divided will, struggling with itself, one part sinking while another rose up.

Finally, in the fever of my hesitation, I made many of those motions with my body that people sometimes would like to, but can't, because their limbs are bound or weakened with infirmity, or are somehow hindered. In this way, if I tore my hair, beat my forehead, or if, locking my fingers together, clasped my knee, I did this because I willed it.

 His body is in convulsions...

I might have willed to do it and yet not done it if the power of motion in my limbs hadn't responded.

I did so many things where to will to do something wasn't the same as having the power to do it, and I didn't do what I longed incomparably more to do. If I had willed thoroughly I could have done it, for then I would have had the power. Power is one with the will, and to will is to do. Yet I didn't do it. My body was more obedient to the slightest wish of my mind in moving its limbs at its direction, than my soul was to obeying itself; this could only be accomplished within the will alone.

Where does this monstrous condition come from? And why? Let your mercy shine on me that I may inquire if the obscurity of humanity's punishments and the darkest feelings of regret for sin of the children of Adam may possibly offer me an answer.

Where does this monstrous condition come from? And why? The mind commands the body, and the body obeys instantly. The mind commands itself and is resisted. The mind commands the hand to be moved, and such readiness is there that you can hardly distinguish the command from its fulfillment. Yet the mind is mind, the hand is body.

The mind commands the mind to will, and yet, though it is itself that commands, it doesn't obey.

Where does this monstrous condition come from? And why? I repeat: It commands itself to will and wouldn't command unless it willed; yet what it commands isn't done. But it doesn't will completely. It doesn't command completely. For so far as it wills it commands, and so far as the thing commanded isn't done it doesn't will. The will commands that there be a will. It doesn't command entirely, therefore what it commands doesn't come about. If the will were sound, it wouldn't even command the will to be, because it would already be. So it isn't strange partly to will and partly to be unwilling, but it's actually an infirmity of the mind, that it can't wholly rise, borne up by truth, but is weighed down by habit. In short, there are two wills, because one isn't sound, and one has what the other lacks.

Let those people perish from your presence, God, as "empty talkers and deceivers" (Titus 1:10 RSV) of the soul perish, who, because they see two wills, claim that there are two natures in us, one good, the other evil. They are truly evil when they hold these evil opinions, and they will become good when they hold the truth and subscribe to the truth, so your apostle may say to them, "you were once darkness, but now you are light in the Lord" (Ephesians 5:8). They, wishing to be light (not in the Lord, but in themselves, imagining the nature of the soul to be the same as God), become thicker darkness. Through their dreadful arrogance they went farther from you, whereas "the true light that gives light to every one was coming into the world" (John 1:9). Take heed what you say, and blush for shame. "Those who look to him are radiant; their faces are never covered with shame" (Psalm 34:5).

Deliberating upon serving the Lord my God at that time, as I had long purposed, it was I who willed, and I who was unwilling. It was I. I neither willed entirely, nor was entirely unwilling. I was therefore at war with myself and torn apart by myself. And this destruction fell on me against my will, yet it didn't show the presence of another mind, but the punishment of my own. Therefore "it is no longer I myself who do it, but sin living in me" (Romans 7:17); I was suffering the punishment of a sin more freely committed, in that I was a child of Adam.

For if there are as many contrary natures as there are conflicting wills, there would now be not only two, but many. If a person deliberates whether they should go to a Manichean meeting or to the theater, the Manicheans cry out, "Observe! Here are two natures: one good, drawing this way; the other bad, drawing back that way. Where else does this hesitation between conflicting wills come from?" I say that both are bad: The nature that which draws them toward the Manicheans is as bad as the one that draws toward the theater. But the Manicheans believe that the will is good that inclines toward them. Suppose that one of us Christians should deliberate, and in the battle of his two wills be in a quandary, whether to go to the theater or to church. Wouldn't these Manicheans also be in a quandary about what to answer? For either they must confess (which they would *not* like to do) that the will that leads to our church is good, or they must suppose two evil natures and two evil minds in conflict within one person, instead of seeing the truth: that in deliberation, one mind fluctuates between conflicting wills.

Let them no longer say when they see two conflicting wills in one person, that the conflict is between two contrary natures, between two opposing substances, from two opposing principles, one good, and the other bad. For you, true God, disprove, check, and convince them by facts. Suppose, for instance, that a person deliberates whether to kill a person by poison or by the sword; whether to seize this or that estate of another's when they can't seize both; whether to purchase pleasure by extravagance or keep their money by stinginess; whether to go to the circus or to the theater, if both are open on the same day, or to make a third choice to rob another's house if they have the opportunity— or, even a fourth one, to commit adultery, if at the same time they have the opportunity. All these, concurring at the same point of time, and all being equally desired, but impossible to do at the same time, tear the mind amid the four or even more conflicting wills. But the Manicheans don't indicate that there are many different substances.

It's the same thing in wills that are good. For I ask them, is it good to take pleasure in reading the apostle, or good to take pleasure in a psalm, or good to discuss the Gospel? They will answer to each, "Yes, it's good." What then, if all give equal pleasure and all are offered at the same time? Do different wills distract the mind while the person deliberates which one to choose? All of them are good, and are at variance until the person chooses one of them, toward which the whole united will may move, this will that was previously divided into several parts.

When eternity gives us great joy and the pleasure of temporal good holds us down, it's the same soul that wills either way with an entire will. Therefore it's torn apart with severe confusion, because its love of truth first shows one way to be preferable, while its habits keep it bound to the other.

I was soul-sick and tormented, accusing myself much more severely than I usually did, tossing and turning in my chain, till it should be utterly broken, for what held me now was trivial. And you, Lord, pressed on me inwardly with severe mercy, redoubling the lashes of fear and shame, for fear that I should give way again and that slight remaining tie, not being broken, should recover its strength and bind me more strongly.

 He's trying to "put his other foot in the boat," but he can't quite do it yet...

I said to myself, "Let it be done now, let it be done now!" And as I spoke, I made a firm resolve, or rather, I almost did it, but didn't.

Yet I didn't sink back to my old condition, but kept my position close enough to get my breath. I tried again, and came very near reaching the point of resolve, then missed it even a little less, and then I all but touched and grasped it. I still didn't quite make it, or touch it, or lay hold of it, hesitating to die to death and to live to life. The worse, to which I had become accustomed, prevailed more with me than the better, which I hadn't tried. And the very moment in which I was to become another person— the nearer it approached me, the greater horror it struck in me. Yet it didn't strike me back utterly or turn me away, but held me in suspense.

The very toys of triviality and emptiness, my old mistresses, still held me. They tugged at the garment of my flesh and whispered softly, "Are you going to part with us? From that moment will we never be with you anymore forever? And from that moment will this or that never be lawful for you forever?" What did they suggest by those words "this or that"? What was it that they suggested, my God? Let your mercy turn it away from the mind of your servant! What defilements they suggested! What shame! But now I didn't hear them half so loudly, for they didn't show themselves openly to contradict me, but muttered, so to speak, behind my back, furtively tugging at me as I was leaving, to make me look back at them. Yet they did delay me, so that I hesitated to burst and shake myself free from them, and to leap over to where I was called to be. An unruly habit kept saying to me, "Do you think that you can live without them?"

But now it was saying this very faintly. For on that side to which I had set my face, where I was trembling to go, the morally pure dignity of Lady Continence appeared to me—serene, not unduly cheerful, honestly bidding me to come and doubt nothing. She extended her holy hands to receive and embrace me, abounding in multitudes of good examples. There were so many young men and women here—a multitude of people of every age, solemn widows and aged virgins; and Continence herself was in all, not barren but a fruitful mother of children of joys by you, her Bridegroom, Lord. She smiled on me with challenging encouragement, as if to say, "Can't you do what these young people, what these women can? Can any of them do it by themselves, and not rather in the Lord their God? The Lord gave me to them. Why do you stand in your own strength and therefore not stand at all? Cast yourself fearlessly upon him; he will receive you and will heal you."

I blushed exceedingly at having listened to the muttering of those trivial toys and hung in indecision. And Lady Continence again seemed to say, "'Put to death, therefore, whatever belongs to your earthly nature' (Colossians 3:5). It tells you of delights, but 'contrary to the law of the Lord your God' (see Psalm 119:85)." This conflict in my heart was self against self only. But Alypius, sitting close by my side in silence, waited the outcome of my unusual emotion.

When my deep self-examination had dredged up from the secret depths of my soul all my misery and piled it up in the sight of my heart, a mighty storm arose, bringing a great shower of tears. To give full vent to them, I got up and left Alypius. Complete solitude seemed to me more appropriate for the business of weeping, so I went far enough away that even his presence couldn't be a hindrance to me. He understood this, for I suppose I said something in which the tone of my voice appeared choked and weeping as I left. He stayed alone where we had been sitting, still completely astonished. I threw myself down, I don't know how, under a certain fig tree, giving full vent to my tears. The streams of my eyes gushed out, an acceptable sacrifice to you (Psalm 51:17).

It wasn't in these words, yet to this purpose that I spoke much to you: "How long, LORD? Will you be angry for ever?"(Psalm 79:5) "Remember not our former iniquities" (Psalm 78:8 D-R [79:8 RSV])? For I felt that I was still held by them. I sent up these sorrowful cries, "How long? How long? Tomorrow and tomorrow? Why not now? Why is there not an end to my impurities this very hour?"

I was speaking this way and weeping in the most bitter contrition of my heart, when suddenly I heard from a neighboring house a voice, as of a boy or girl, I don't know which—chanting repeatedly, "Take up and read. Take up and read."

 He hears a mysterious and unseen child's voice...

My facial expression changed instantly, and I began to think most earnestly whether children were in the habit of playing any kind of game with such words. I couldn't remember ever having heard anything like it. So checking the torrent of my tears, I got up, interpreting this to be nothing other than a command from God to open the Book and to read the first chapter I would find. For I heard of Antony, that he had come into church during the reading of these words in the Gospel, "Go, sell your possessions and give to the poor, and you will have treasure in heaven. Then come, follow me" (Matthew 19:21). He had received these words as addressed to himself, and by such a revelation was immediately converted to you.

So I quickly returned to the place where Alypius was sitting, where I had laid the volume of the Apostle. I grabbed it, opened it, and in silence read the paragraph on which my eyes first fell: "Not in carousing and drunkenness, not in sexual immorality and debauchery, not in dissension and jealousy. Rather, clothe yourselves with the Lord Jesus Christ, and do not think about how to gratify the desires of the sinful nature" (Romans 13:13-14). I read no further, nor did I need to. For instantly, at the end of this sentence, it was as if a light of peaceful calm and quietness poured into my heart, and all the darkness of doubt vanished away.

 He converts...or, is converted.

Closing the book, and putting my finger between the pages, I told Alypius about it with a calm look on my face. He asked to look at what I had read. I showed him, and he read on even further than I had (I didn't know what followed). There it was written, "accept the person whose faith is weak" (Romans 14:1). He applied this word to himself and showed it to me. He was strengthened by this admonition, and by a good resolution and purpose, which was very much in accord with his character (he was far different from me and far better), without any restless delay, he joined me.

Then we went in to my mother and told her, relating in order how all these events took place. She leapt for joy, expressed delight, and praised you, who are "able to do immeasurably more than all we ask or imagine" (Ephesians 3:20). She knew that you had given her more in me than she had been praying for by her pitiful and sorrowful groanings.

 ...and he tells his mother that her prayers have been answered.

You converted me to yourself, so that I was no longer seeking a wife or any other hope of worldly success—I was standing firm on that rule of faith on which you showed me to her in a vision so many years before [see page 71]. You turned her grief into a much more plentiful gladness than she had desired, and in a much dearer and purer way than she used to crave when she asked for grandchildren.

Library
Benedictine University Mesa

A Final Note

You've just read the first eight books of Augustine's *Confessions*, and they are the most famous. But you should know that the books do go on. In book nine, Augustine writes of his Christian baptism (with his best friend, Alypius, and his sixteen-year-old son, Adeodatus) and his abandonment of the study and teaching of rhetoric. He also writes of the deaths of his close friends Nebridius and Vecundus, the death of his sainted mother, Monica, who died of a fever just days after Augustine's conversion, and the death of his son, Adeodatus, at age eighteen.

Augustine clearly had very close relationships and very strong feelings for these friends, and for his mother and his son. Reminiscing about their deaths in book nine leads to a long and complicated meditation on memory in book ten, a book that philosophers have studied closely for centuries. Finally, books eleven through thirteen are more explicitly theological, exploring the book of Genesis and the meaning of the Trinity.

Although the *Confessions* only track Augustine's life until his early thirties, and he wrote them in his late forties, he lived until the age of seventy-six and authored hundreds of sermons, letters, and books. He is widely regarded as the most important theologian, after St. Paul, in the history of the Western church.

About Paraclete Press

Who We Are

Paraclete Press is an ecumenical publisher of books and recordings on Christian spirituality. Our publishing represents a full expression of Christian belief and practice—from Catholic to Evangelical, from Protestant to Orthodox. Paraclete Press is the publishing arm of the Community of Jesus, an ecumenical monastic community in the Benedictine tradition. As such, we are uniquely positioned in the marketplace without connection to a large corporation and with informal relationships to many branches and denominations of faith.

We like it best when people buy our books from booksellers, our partners in successfully reaching as wide an audience as possible.

What We Are Doing

Books

Paraclete Press publishes books that show the richness and depth of what it means to be Christian. Although Benedictine spirituality is at the heart of all that we do, we publish books that reflect the Christian experience across many cultures, time periods, and houses of worship.

We publish books that nourish the vibrant life of the church and its people–books about spiritual practice, formation, history, ideas, and customs.

We have several different series of books within Paraclete Press, including the bestselling Living Library series of modernized classic texts; A Voice from the Monastery—giving voice to men and women monastics about what it means to live a spiritual life today; award winning literary faith fiction; and books that explore Judaism and Islam and discover how these faiths inform Christian thought and practice.

Recordings

From Gregorian chant to contemporary American choral works, our music recordings celebrate the richness of sacred choral music through the centuries. Paraclete is proud to distribute the recordings of the internationally acclaimed choir Gloriæ Dei Cantores, who have been praised for their "rapt and fathomless spiritual intensity" by American Record Guide, and the Gloriæ Dei Cantores Schola, which specializes in the study and performance of Gregorian chant. Paraclete is also the exclusive North American distributor of the Monastic Choir of St. Peter's Abbey in Solesmes, France, long considered to be a leading authority on Gregorian chant performance.

Learn more about us at our Web site:
www.paracletepress.com, or call us toll-free at
1-800-451-5006.

ALSO AVAILABLE FROM PARACLETE PRESS

*"We are very close to accepting God
as the only source of meaning."*

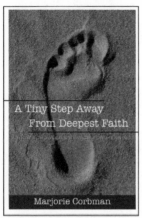

A Tiny Step Away from Deepest Faith:

A Teenager's Search for Meaning
Marjorie Corbman

101 pages, Trade Paper
ISBN: 1-55725-429-X
$9.95

So says eighteen-year old Marjorie
Corbman in this passionate search
for God, love, and identity. Marjorie
dismantles with transparency and
grace the misconceptions surround-
ing today's teenagers. Honest and engaging, she charts her own
transformations, from growing up in a home with little interest
in spiritual things to her own preparations for conversion. Along
the way, she discusses intimacy, tradition, eternity, community,
justice, escape—and how each relates to what Marjorie calls the
only thing necessary—faith.

"Corbman offers readers a rare and thought-provoking gem: the
story of a teenage girl struggling with life's biggest questions
about meaning, love, suffering, loneliness, and most of all, God.
Her story will resonate not because it sounds authentically young
adult, but because she is a young adult herself, still searching.
She differs only in that she has found a surer spiritual footing
than most her age."

—*Publishers Weekly*

Available from most booksellers or through Paraclete Press
www.paracletepress.com
1-800-451-5006 • Try your local bookstore first.